♥ **Where i**

This book is inspired by a blog I v
a mother dog and her litter of sev
home, the pups were merely three weeks old. By the time the final two left, our two week temporary foster had turned into three months.

When you volunteer for rescues by fostering animals, they usually encourage you to share lots of pictures and information about the animals to make them seem more personable and hopefully increase their likelihood of being adopted. As a writer, I had the idea of starting a blog, where I could share stories of the animals along with photos and hopefully tackle two issues rescue organizations face: finding people to adopt animals, and inspiring others to foster animals.

My blog posts were shared on the rescue's Facebook page and it generated a lot of comments and positive feedback. The blog did help with the ultimate goal, which was to get this family adopted into their own homes.

Another thing happened, though. My rescue colleagues were suggesting my blog could be used to create a book on fostering. It was a good idea. A really good idea. And I'm embarrassed to say that it has taken me four years to move ahead with that idea.

This book includes my original blog posts, with some edits, including removing the name of the rescue organization and those associated with it. This was done for two reasons. First, the organization no longer exists. Second, my tale ends with a cautionary note of doing some research before diving into volunteering with a rescue.

Reading through my old blog posts has made me laugh, and cry, and sometimes even long to foster again. Most of all, it has made me grateful - grateful for the experience, and grateful to still be in contact with some of the families who adopted Valley and her pups. My only regret is that I am not connected with them all.

This book is written for:

- Anyone fostering animals for an animal rescue
- Anyone considering fostering animals for an animal rescue
- Animal rescues
- Animal rescue volunteers
- Anyone who loves animals

I do not pretend to be an expert at anything regarding dogs. I am simply a person who loves animals - dogs in particular - and who, along with the love of my life, was able to experience the highs (and lows) of fostering a family of dogs for an animal rescue.

While this book is primarily written with dog fostering in mind, much of what I have written could be adapted and applied as appropriate for other animals, be it cats, rabbits, hamsters, potbelly pigs, horses, or llamas - pretty much anything. Well, some aspects would need to be tweaked, obviously.

Important note: I am not a lawyer. I am not a dog trainer. I am not a veterinarian. I am not a sociologist or a psychologist. I am a writer. I am a lover of dogs. This book is a culmination of my knowledge and experience. It not to be considered legal or veterinary advice, it is not to be considered training advice. At most, I hope it inspires you to support rescues, whether to donate, foster, or adopt. I hope you enjoy our story.

♥ Shout Outs

Indulge me as I thank those who helped bring this vision to life:

To my family and friends: thank you for all your kindness and support once I got it in my head that it was time to finally write this book.

To those who donated: thank you for believing in me so much that you actually contributed towards the cost of printing this book.

To my friend, Dixie: thank you for giving me the extra nudge I needed to get things going, for reading the first draft, and for your sage advice.

To Liz and Chelsea: thank you for pushing and prodding me years ago to turn my blog into a book, for your support while we were fostering, and for everything you have done over the years.

Jennifer: I owe you a special thank you for coining the phrase, "knee deep in puppy poop" in response to one of my early blog posts. As you can see, the phrase stuck. To Joan, thank you for giving my book a shout out and for inspiring me with your own foster story. You both have the kindest hearts and are special souls.

And finally, thank you to my husband, Terry, who I love more and more each day, who probably should tell me "no" more often, especially when I ask questions like "Can we foster these dogs?" or "Can we adopt this puppy?" or "Can we adopt two potbelly pigs?"

Knee Deep in Puppy Poop
The Story Begins ...

Blog: Adventures in Puppy Fostering

How could I have known an innocent re-post of an animal rescue looking for a foster for a dog and her seven 3-week old puppies would result in ME being that foster??

It has to be known that Sarge and I are dog enthusiasts – it is one of the reasons we knew we were meant to be together, as we both dream of winning the lottery so we can build a dog rescue ranch.

But with our own pack in a small duplex, fostering seemed out of the realm of possibility - until a temporary foster opportunity came about.

So as of 11:00 this morning, in addition to my own brat pack, I have a lovely dog named Valentina and her seven puppies staying with us. As she is a dog from a reserve, she is not accustomed to many things my spoiled babies take for granted. For instance, this is her first time ever in a house – seriously! She has never seen stairs before, and although she has mastered going up them (with a little coaxing with raw hot dogs), I do need to carry her back down to the basement to be with her puppies.

oh.my.god.the puppies. If they inherit their mother's temperament, they will be seven of the nicest dogs you can ever imagine. They have already inherited her unique puppy smile. It's too adorable for words.

Bringing these guys into the home at three weeks will be an interesting adventure as they are just now getting their baby teeth, have learned that they can bark and growl, and are starting to play. Instead of fat lazy babies that eat and sleep, I have the responsibility – and the pleasure – of socializing them and making them ready to be adopted into new homes.

I think Sarge n' I are up to the challenge.

In the meantime, my own brat pack are separated from momma and the babies, and they are seriously pissed with me as they want to investigate the source of the new smells and sounds in the house. Oh well, sucks to be them. Special thanks to the rescue team who has already done so much to get us set up and on our way. Let the adventure begin!

Jumping in with Both Feet

The foster application, home checks, and the foster agreement

I don't think it was ever in the forefront of our minds that my husband, Terry (a.k.a. Sarge) and I would ever volunteer for an animal rescue by fostering dogs. I can certainly say it was not a topic we had ever discussed. And there is no way we ever discussed bringing in an adult dog with seven puppies into our small home when we already had four dogs of our own. That conversation happened very quickly one evening when I saw a post on Facebook from a local rescue needing someone to take in this family for a couple of weeks.

What's a couple of weeks, right?

After responding to the post that we would, in fact, be willing to take in this family, our life became a flurry of activity. I was immediately contacted by the rescue and asked questions about our home: where were we planning to keep them, did we have dogs, did we have kids, did we have a fenced yard, how high was the fence, how long are we away from home during the day, etc.

Apparently we gave all the right answers as the rescue quickly agreed to allow us to foster Valley and her pups – well, pending a home check the next morning. The head of the rescue came to the house first to check everything out. I showed her the yard, the basement where we were going to keep the family, and introduced her to our own dog family (a.k.a. the "brat pack") to assure her of their temperaments. About an hour later, a rescue volunteer showed up with Valley and the pups and we were in business.

Because ours was supposed to only be a temporary foster situation until a more permanent foster could be found, the review and approval process wasn't as rigorous as it normally would have been. Being new to the situation, we also didn't know what questions to ask and didn't even think about agreements or contracts. Hindsight is 20/20, and I learned that was not exactly our smartest move, and yet it did work to our advantage when puppy poop hit the fan.

If you are considering fostering with a serious and reputable rescue, you can expect three things: a foster application, a home check, and a foster agreement

The Foster Application

Be prepared to answer, at minimum, questions about you, your home, and your commitment. Depending on the rescue, there may be even more questions. And if you aren't asked at least the following questions – or any questions at all – approach with caution.

What type of residence do you have – house, apartment, townhouse, acreage, condo?

Do you rent or own your home? If you rent – do you have express written permission from your landlord to bring an animal into your home? Be prepared to provide this written consent to the rescue. The last thing they need is you calling in a couple weeks saying you have to give up the foster as your landlord doesn't allow dogs or cats.

Do you live in a condo or in a residential development with a homeowners' association (HOA)? If so, are there animal restrictions, including height and/or breed restrictions? You may need to check your condominium bylaws or homeowner association regulations. In some cases, you can appeal to the condo board or HOA for an exemption, which I have seen granted in some cases. Do your research and make the necessary applications as may be required. The adage "it's better to beg for forgiveness than to ask for permission" does not go over so well with condo boards, HOAs, and municipal governments.

Who will be the primary caregiver? Is the primary caregiver over the age of 18 years? This is important as some rescues may require you to sign a foster agreement or contract and that person needs to be of legal age to get into these agreements.

Identify all persons in the home including adults and children. Some rescues will ask the sex of the individuals in the home, particularly for placement of animals that may have issues with certain people (e.g. fearful of men, not good with children, etc.) You may also be asked if all residents – particularly the adults – agree to foster an animal. This is very important as fostering a single animal – or a whole family – will impact your household.

Do you have a fenced yard? If so, be prepared to describe the height of the fence, what it is made of, and even the condition of the fence. Some rescues will not permit fostering in homes without fenced yards, and many will not accept electric or "invisible" fences.

If you don't have a fenced yard, you may be asked how you will plan to exercise the dog and where it would do its business. This is particularly important if you live on the 15th floor of an apartment and have only a small deck. What will you do at 3 a.m. if the dog needs to pee?

You may be asked whether you have your own transportation, and, if you do, if you are willing and able to transport the animal to vet appointments and/or adoption events. Not having a vehicle isn't necessarily a deal-breaker – it just helps the rescue know if they need to work with you to arrange alternative transportation for these situations.

Expect to be asked about your daily routine, particularly how long you would typically be away from the home, leaving the foster alone. If you are gone for 12 hours a day, and there's no one else to check in, you may not be the ideal foster for a dog.

What is your experience with animals? Note: fostering isn't always the best introduction to pet ownership. Often times, animals coming into care have been dumped, abandoned, or surrendered due to behavioural issues, and may require more experienced pet owners. That said, there are also many well-behaved animals surrendered for other reasons, including family illness, divorce, or death. Being honest in your answer can help ensure the rescue matches you with the right foster.

What is your foster commitment? Are you willing to foster long-term, until adoption? Or are you looking for short term, for example, to cover another foster going on vacation?

Be prepared to answer questions regarding your style for training and discipline. Again, be honest in your answers as this is to ensure the best foster match and for the safety of you and the animal.

What are the bylaws in your community for number of permitted animals? This is an important question and needs to be on every application. If your community only allows two dogs per household, and you already have two as dogs as pets, unless there are provisions in the bylaw stating otherwise, bringing in a foster will put you over the limit and you can be subject to fines, which the rescue likely will not pay. Plus the rescue will need to take back the foster and try to find another home, which can put undue stress on the rescue and the animal.

If you are serious about fostering, check with your municipality to see how you can do this legally, for example, applying for a dog kennel permit.

And, finally, what age of animal are you interested in fostering – puppy or adult? Think long and hard about this one. Puppies are cute. And a lot of work.

Look closely at your home, your life, your family – are you set up for little ankle-biters that need to be housebroken, or are you better off with an older dog that is just looking for a temporary home. Not only are puppies a lot of work, but you are also preparing them for someone else to adopt, which is an even greater responsibility.

Blog: Knee Deep in Puppy Poop

It is surprising how much those little guys poop. And because they all eat at the same time, they almost poop simultaneously. Actually, not quite. It goes like this.

While I am cleaning the pen, the pups all scramble about the rest of the basement and each takes a turn, one right after the other, making additional "deposits" in various parts of the basement, basically leaving me the challenge of dodging puppy landmines. Fun!

The puppies are growing fast and are learning how to play. They are also having fun trying out their new teeth. Not so fun for my toes, their newly-found chew toy. Their personalities are also coming out more, although Vespa is still the one who stands out the most, mainly because she makes sure you notice her!

Valley has come a long way as well. She hangs upstairs with us, relaxing and enjoying a break from seven demanding puppies. She has also stopped following us around everywhere, which, in my mind, suggests she is more comfortable. She even started playing a bit when she goes outside, which is really wonderful to see. It's a happy little home.

The Home Check

If you've passed the application stage, then you can expect a home visit. This is the rescue's opportunity to confirm what you said in your application, get to know you and anyone else living with you, and - if you pass the inspection - assess the type of animal that would be most appropriate for you to foster.

This is also your opportunity to assess the rescue. Here are some tips to help you get ready for the home check.

Research, research, research. Visit their website. Visit their Facebook page. Read the reviews. Google the rescue's name. Search for Instagram or other social media accounts. Read the comments, both good and bad. Look for trends, but keep an open mind.

You may find complaints like "they wouldn't adopt a dog to me" or "their adoption fees are too high." A reputable organization will have a rigorous adoption program to ensure the right animal is placed in the right home. If people are rejected, there is often a reason why.

Rescues also run on donations and adoption fees, and those fees barely cover veterinary costs, including vaccinations and spay/neutering, much less all the food and supplies provided to the foster families while the animal is in care.

Look at the adoption application and the fees and ask yourself "are they being unreasonable in what they are asking?"

If you are seeing multiple posts on their Facebook page from other foster families begging for someone from the rescue to contact them, that they need help, no one is answering their phone calls, etc., this could be a warning sign and you may want to cancel the home check.

Prepare your own questions. Think of any scenario that could happen, any questions you might have, write them down, and be sure to ask them. Sample questions include:

- Who pays for the dog food? Where do they get it from?
- What if you run out and have to buy supplies, who reimburses? How? Do you need pre-approval before you buy anything?
- What happens if the dog gets sick or hurt? What vet do they use? Do they have to get approval from the rescue first, or can you just take the dog in?
- What happens if you have an emergency and need someone to take the dog?
- What if the dog isn't adopted after a certain length of time?

- What if you want to keep the dog (also known as a "foster fail") – do you have to pay the full adoption fee, or will they waive it?

- What happens if the foster hurts your dog (or cat, or hamster) – do they cover the vet bills? What if your pet hurts the foster – do you have to cover the vet bill?

- What if the foster attacks a dog at the off leash park? Do you even have permission to take the dog to an off leash park?

- What supports are available to you to help with the foster if necessary, e.g. dog trainers, groomers?

- What if you are going away on business or vacation – can someone you choose stay with the dog, or do they find another foster home? What happens if they can't find another foster home?

These are only *some* of the questions you should ask. Consider your own situation. When you meet with the rescue, be sure you are comfortable with the answers. Write them down, and ensure they are all addressed in the next step: the Foster Agreement.

The Foster Agreement

While you were researching the rescue, there is the possibility that you might have come across their foster agreement – if they make it public. If not, ask for a copy in advance of the home check. This will give you an opportunity to read it in advance and understand their requirements as well as check to see which of your questions have – and have not – been addressed in the agreement.

It's not a big deal if you don't get the document in advance of the home check - that's just a "nice to have." The important things are:

- They actually have an agreement

- You are given sufficient time to review it

- You are not asked to sign it without reading it first

If you have questions or concerns that aren't addressed in the agreement, ask to have the agreement amended to include them. This is particularly important for situations where you could become personally or financially liable.

Remember: an agreement is a form of contract and the expectation is both parties live up to their end of that agreement. Where you live determines if the agreement is legal and valid. For the most part, unless there are parts of the agreement that cannot be enforced due to local laws, the balance of the agreement can still be enforced. This includes any actions that the rescue may take against you – or you against the rescue. If you aren't comfortable signing the agreement, and the rescue isn't willing to amend it, you may want to walk away. There are many other rescues and many other animals looking for people like you.

But enough of the negative. Fostering an animal can be a very rewarding and enjoyable experience. I just wanted to make sure you are jumping in with your eyes open and your butt covered.

Blog: I want to be the person my dog thinks I am

Since volunteering to foster for a rescue, the question most asked of Sarge and me is why would you do something for which you don't get paid?

Because it makes the heart feel good to do something good for someone else, especially for an animal – be it a dog or a cat or whatever – that is in need. And somehow these animals know you're doing something special and they let you know how much they appreciate it. That's payment enough.

Why would you voluntarily take on so much extra work?

When you already have pets, one more (or two more!) isn't that much extra work. Sure, when we had a momma and seven puppies, things were challenging. But they reward you in spades.

Why would you keep a dog or cat that you can't keep? Isn't it tough letting go?

I cried when I said goodbye to Valley and the pups when they found homes. But it was more out of happiness for them that they were getting their own home, a happy life where they are cared for and get to be the centre of a family's world. I wasn't sad to see them go – I was happy for them.

Some days I am tired and question my sanity as I step around my mini-herd of pets and fosters. But then I sit down and a sweet little face looks up at me, and it reminds me everything I do makes their life that much better. Ever hear the saying "I want to be the person my dog thinks I am?" Well, fostering MAKES me that person.

Blog: Puppy Mayhem

This morning, when my furbabies woke me at 4 a.m to let them out, I also went to the basement to get Valley. A picture is worth a thousand words, but grabbing the camera was the last thing on my mind.

The wire puppy pen has a door, and the rise to the door is quite low, easy for the puppies to get over. As a temporary measure, I had put some plastic slats across to keep the puppies in but keeping it low enough for Valley to get in and out.

The temporary measure proved how temporary it was.

I opened the door to find Valley laying in the middle of the floor. There were puppies in the pen, puppies in Valley's kennel, puppies outside the pen attacking Valley's dish of puppy kibble. The floor was littered with pumpkin-orange puppy poops, smushed from the water of Valley's tipped-over water dish. The slats were cast aside, a tribute to their ineffectiveness. The puppies were in their glory; Valley and me – not so much.

Oh hell.

I brought Valley upstairs so she could go outside and do her thing. I grabbed some paper towel, then she and I set back downstairs to re-assess the damage.

Being a good momma, she quickly laid down away from the mess so her squawking babies could have a snack while I cleaned up. I scanned the room for something to replace the broken slats, another temporary fix while I waited until daylight for a permanent fix. It has to be said that 4 a.m. is not my best time for problem-solving. With nothing leaping out at me, I instead set out to puppy-proof the rest of the basement.

Yes, I was tired and I was frustrated, but with myself – not them. But it is hard to stay grumpy with seven little puppies surrounding you, licking toes and ankles, looking up with happy little faces, fat little bums wiggling their cute little tails, making their funny little baby puppy barks.

All is forgiven.

When I woke up at a more decent hour, I went back downstairs to see how bad things had gotten in the last three hours. Thankfully, the puppies had behaved themselves, although still convinced Valley's kibble was for them. I placed them back in their pen, miraculously found a board to cover the door, gave them their pumpkin mixture, and set about my day. I think Valentina was relieved that they were once again contained – poor girl needs a break too!

2 Preparing to Foster
Setting up your home, your pets, and your life

If ever I thought I was prepared to foster animals, I was wrong. Very wrong. Not in a bad way, but I am hoping my experience and lessons learned are valuable to you and help you be much better prepared.

My first reality check occurred during the home check and the conversation in the basement where we had planned to keep Valley and the pups. The rescue organizer looked at the basement window and expressed her concern that Valley might break out through the window.

Wait - what?

The idea seemed a little absurd and I was more than a little surprised that this could be an issue. But then again, I had little experience with rescue dogs, and Valley and her pups were currently living in a garage and she had never been in a house.

She was quite insistent that we should look at blocking off the window, that they had this happen before, where the dog panicked and broke out of the house through the basement window, scaled a six-foot fence, and ran away. We assured her we would pay very close attention to Valley and watch for any signs of stress and anxiety that might cause her to flee her puppies and escape.

It was definitely an eye-opening moment.

Thankfully, we had nothing to worry about in that regard, but it is an important lesson that preparing your home for your foster could mean more than just putting out a bed and a food dish.

Setting up your home

A good rescue will work with you to evaluate what you need and help you get set up with the appropriate supplies. Depending on the situation, this can mean providing kennels, food dishes, toys, collars and leashes. Because we were fostering puppies as well, they also gave us wire pens to keep the puppies contained in one area within the basement (in theory).

If you are considering being a frequent foster, you may want to purchase your own kenneling and pen supplies. Rescues don't always have a vast selection of equipment and it becomes a "take what you can get" situation. Having your own supplies means you can customize for your own home needs and you don't have to worry about returning them to the rescue afterwards.

Quite often, the rescue will supply you with dog food so you are not paying out of pocket. This is the ideal situation. However, they are operating from donations, and sometimes money can get scarce. Hopefully, you won't have to purchase supplies, but if you do, make sure you find out where they buy from. Often times, they have negotiated discount rates with different veterinarians and pet stores for food and other supplies, so it is generally better to go through those channels.

Some rescues will be quite particular about the type of food they feed to their animals - this is something you need to know in advance. Don't expect to be able to get away with low grade dog food when they want you to feed them premium food. Abiding by these requirements is particularly important for animals with food allergies or illnesses that require special diets.

If you do end up buying food to contribute to the animal's care, keep the receipts. If the rescue is a registered charity, you may be able to claim the food as a donation (check with your jurisdiction's tax laws).

Many rescues will recommend keeping the dog in a kennel, and people can have strong opinions about this. From my personal experience with my own dogs and my foster crew, kennels will help save your sanity, your floors, your furniture, and help the dog be a better pet. All my dogs (except my seniors) are kenneled when we aren't home. This keeps them out of trouble and also reduces their stress and anxiety (especially my schnauzer). They are never put in the kennel for punishment; instead, that is where they get their treats and they get excited when I tell them to go to their house.

Whether it is your dog or a foster dog, the kennel becomes a sanctuary, a place to get away from kids and loud noises, a place to nap, their own safe space. It also becomes a helpful house-training tool and reduces accidents in the house. Just be sure the kennel is closed properly!

Blog: Puppy-Gate

This is a story of determination, persistence, a commitment to a cause.

In short, this is a story about Vespa.

Vespa is one of the three female pups in the litter, and although not the smallest (that honour belongs to Vixen), she is also not the largest (that would be Violet). However, Vespa is the most determined, the most curious, and, as far as I can tell, she is the smartest of the litter. This puppy is not for someone who wants a quiet companion laying at his or her feet. Rather, this is a puppy for someone who wants a running companion, someone who likes to hike and is as curious about the world as she is ... someone who would love to take her to dog agility classes!

Vespa. After dealing with escaping puppies, I had to put up a temporary barrier to keep the puppies in their pen. That worked – well, except for Vespa. We then cut a board that was another two inches higher than the temporary barrier. That helped. Except for Vespa.

In fact, we had to put a pillow on the floor on the other side so she would have a soft landing when she crawled over. Make the barrier higher? We would – except Valley wouldn't be able to get over (she's already having to take a jump to cross).

I'm quite convinced that Vespa has either taunted or taught the others to climb over the board as there were random puppies outside of the pen every time I checked on them last night and this morning. I think it is time to give up on trying to keep them in the pen and puppy-proof the basement instead.

I'm going to need a lot more newspaper.

Setting up your pets

Being our first foster experience, we were rather naive about what we needed to do to prepare our dogs for the situation. Us being us, our first experience couldn't be easy. Nope. We had to dive in head-first with a mother dog rescued from a remote area, where she had lived outside for most - if not all - of her life, scavenged for food, and generally saw other dogs as a threat. Add to this a litter of puppies, and you can imagine this could be a potentially volatile situation. Although naive, we are also thankfully logical and intelligent, and considered all of this when setting up the space for Valley and the pups.

Our pack consists of three neutered males and a fixed female. All were socialized with other dogs, and were frequent visitors of the off leash park and

doggie day care. Generally, we had no concerns, but knew that, regardless of how friendly our dogs were, Valentina may still see them as a threat.

We also had to be cautious with our female dog, Sport. As lovely and sweet as she is, she is also a protector, and females can get pretty ornery with each other (no doubt why the term bitch isn't just reserved for female dogs). The last thing we needed was Sport and Valley getting into it.

Proceed with caution.

We knew Valley and the pups would be stationed in the basement and have that space all to themselves. When they arrived, we made sure our pack was locked upstairs so Valley could come inside without being subjected to overly enthusiastic meet and greets. She was shown the back yard where she would be doing her business, and set her up in the basement with her kennel, food, water, and her babies. Our focus was getting her settled as she really was the "unknown" in this canine equation.

When our brat pack was set loose, we did our best to keep them from the basement door. But dogs being dogs, they did sneak down now and again and the loud sniffs spoke to their intense curiosity of what was hiding behind the door. When we finally let Valentina out to meet the family, we kept our pack under control and let them all introduce themselves as dogs do - lots of butt sniffing and checking each other out. With nary a squabble in sight, we knew we had success.

We haven't fostered since, but I have friends that foster both cats and dogs and they have established an excellent routine to prepare their pets for new fosters. This includes setting out foster-specific beds and dishes a few days in advance as a signal to the pet that someone new will be coming home soon. Where possible, the dogs are introduced outside of the home in neutral territory so they can check each other out without the resident dog becoming territorial. Her home also includes cats, which is great as many potential adopters are looking for dogs that are comfortable around cats. She's done a great job.

For cat fosters, because of the potential for very contagious and dangerous feline diseases, my friend has a quarantine space set up in her spare bathroom. A couple of days before the new foster arrives, she will set everything up in the bathroom and close the door so the cats are used to it when the foster is contained in there. After a few days of paws battling from under the door, the quarantine is lifted, and the foster cat joins the family. It has worked very well for her and she has a number of successful adoptions – and a couple of foster fails – under her belt.

So now you have your home ready and your pets ready - are you ready?

Blog: Puppy Steps

As much as this experience is about fostering puppies, it is also about their momma learning about a whole new world, and it is about us coming to a new understanding of helping those who cannot help themselves.

Within a few short hours of joining our household, Valentina (who I have already nicknamed Valley-Girl), has fallen in love with Terry. In fact, while he was re-stringing his bass guitar, she was staring at him and smiling with her awesome puppy smile. She grins like no other dog I've seen. Her crush on him was also evidenced last night after he came home from his jam, went to let her out and visit, and promptly had her curl up and fall asleep on his chest. They both dozed off, cuddled together for about 40 minutes.

Valley has also taken other huge steps. She is no longer afraid of the stairs, and goes up and down easily without prompting (well, she does like it if we lead the way). She was also introduced to the rest of the clan today and was quickly smiling and wagging her tail. I think she likes being around "grown-ups" for a change.

Our clan is happy to have met her, but they know we are still holding out on them, especially since we won't let them go downstairs to where the puppies are …

And, as always, back to the puppies!! Yesterday, they had their first solid food meal, which was an interesting mixture of pumpkin, cottage cheese, and plain yogurt. They went nuts for it!!! Who'd have thought that puppies would love pumpkin, yogurt and cottage cheese!

Blog: Text from Sarge

Sarge: Aaaaaaaaaaaaaaaaaaahhhhhh!!!!

Me: Uh oh. Good morning!

Sarge: THEY GOT OUT!!!

Me: Oh no!!!!!!

Sarge: Clean up is going to be the whole basement tonight. The door was open.

Me: Must not have closed the pins all the way.

Sarge: Yes I did. That's the shocker I even double checked.

Apparently the pups are getting good at destroying the basement. But it doesn't end there. Later that evening ...

Sarge: They are quiet. I'm scared.

Me: LOL

Sarge: Let the fun begin ... (he heads down to clean basement).

Sarge: OMG! They got out again! Just finished downstairs now have to clean upstairs! They are making me work!

Me: LOL Sorry I can't stop laughing. I feel so bad for you.

Sarge: Even with my cleaning it's still pretty ugly. Oh gawd I hear them moving. Shhhh maybe they won't hear me.

At that point, I was laughing so hard, I couldn't even text him any longer. Because of the sheer size of these puppies, when they push on the wire pen, it causes the pins to slide open, which opens the door and they get out. We resolved this by putting the coffee table in front and it keeps things stable. Safely contained within their pen, all was right in the world again. For now ...

Setting up your Life

One of the key questions in the foster application is ensuring all in the household are supportive of the foster situation. Whether a single animal or a whole family, fostering is a big commitment that will have an impact on your life, from caring for the animal, to vet appointments, meet and greets, and adoption events. Everyone in the home really needs to be on board.

I didn't need to talk Sarge into fostering. All I had to do was show him the picture of Valley and the pups and he immediately agreed. We both knew that I was likely to be the primary caregiver, but I also knew that I would have his full support as needed.

Our initial commitment was for a couple of weeks and neither of us had anything going on within that timeframe. But as the rescue was challenged with trying to find a new foster home, that two weeks extended to three ... then four. We were okay with it, but it also meant that Terry was going to have to look after the house, our dogs, and the foster family when I had to go away for work.

All of this would have been impossible – or at least a serious challenge to our relationship – if we were not both completely on board with fostering.

I would caution against viewing fostering as an opportunity for kids to learn about the responsibility of having pets. While it can be a good introduction, it is quite unique in that you are preparing the dog for someone else to adopt, which requires you to follow rules and guidelines that you may not follow with your own pet.

That said, having a family shouldn't prevent you from fostering. As long as the primary responsibility for care and training remains with the adults, it can be an opportunity to share duties with children and take some of the pressure off the parents.

Blog: They scare me when they sleep

The pups have become very social and extremely playful. When you enter the pen, it is puppy pounces and barks and total playtime. I have to be careful to close the basement door as they have figured out how to climb the stairs and they no longer want to be in the basement. They are still too young and their bodies are still forming for them to be climbing stairs. So this means carrying them. Upstairs. And back downstairs. And they're getting big. And heavy.

When upstairs, they want to chase me, Terry and the brat pack, who are slowly becoming more accustomed to the rambunctious youngsters. There is no ignoring this bunch when they have it in their mind to play. Don't leave anything on the floor or hanging because it is immediately converted to a toy.

I look around and see them all fast asleep, sprawled out in various parts of the living room, some with twitchy feet as they run with their dreams, others let out the occasional bark, whimper or whine. But mostly all is calm, quiet. And as I watch them sleep, I realize they are simply building up more energy to start the attack anew.

God help me ... one of them just woke up ...

Bringing up mom & babies
Feeding, growing, and veterinary care

Feeding

If you've ever been in a pet store, you know there is a vast selection of dog foods from which to choose, with food for puppies to active adults, from seniors to overweight dogs. But nowhere is there a dog food for nursing mothers.

Thankfully, we had direction from the rescue as to what to feed Valentina: a high quality puppy kibble. Not only is puppy kibble recommended for nursing moms, but it helped make a difference for the poor girl who was underweight and having to feed seven very hungry and growing puppies.

Once the puppies were weaned, we transitioned her to adult food, first starting off mixing half and half, then slowing reducing the puppy kibble until she was on adult food alone. Using the same brand of food and mixing the two resulted in less gastrointestinal upsets. Anyone who has suffered canine farts after switching dog food knows the pain.

As for feeding the puppies, our assumption – which I am sure you would echo – was that all the feeding would be done by Valentina. Our assumption was wrong.

The rescue organizer advised that, because these were larger breed dogs, it was time to start introducing some solid foods into the pups' diet. This would help accomplish three things: help them grow, become accustomed to solids, and help Valentina gain weight as they would nurse less. What was more curious was what we were asked to feed them: a slurry that consisted of equal parts cottage cheese, yogurt and canned pumpkin.

Who feeds a dog pumpkin?

Turns out, pumpkin is great for dogs, especially those having tummy troubles, and is great for resolving diarrhea. They also like it. A lot. In fact, in the fall when I break up whole pumpkins for my potbelly pigs, it is a race between them and the dogs to get a chunk. It's really quite funny.

The puppies also enjoyed it, and for the first couple of weeks with us, they were given their pumpkin-yogurt-cottage cheese mix twice a day to augment what they were getting from mom. When we moved into the third week, we started adding puppy kibble to the mix, letting it soften first, then giving to the puppies, getting them accustomed to it.

The only downside was the orange-tinged puppy poop. And there were times

17

when I felt I was knee deep in that orange puppy poop.

Slowly, we reduced the ratio of pumpkin-yogurt-cottage cheese to kibble, until it was a mere dollop, much like whip cream on a pie. Eventually, the puppies were eating kibble alone and continued to grow … and grow … and grow …

Blog: Humour and Exhaustion

My favourite moment of the week was Friday, when Sarge had to take care of the pups after work. I understand it happened like this: Terry goes down to clean pen and feed the "starving" beasts. After taking care of those duties, he goes back upstairs and heads outside to take care of the big dogs' mess in the backyard. He had closed the pen, but left the basement door open so Valley could come in and out at her leisure. He also left the patio door open so Valley and the rest of the brat pack could come in and out.

Good plan. Or not. I get the following text message from him:

"So I'm letting the dogs outside and all of a sudden I hear this strange noise. It's all the pups coming up the stairs. With absolutely no problem. Had to panic while writing this, forgot the door was open and four of them got out."

The pups are now over six weeks old and they are extremely curious about the world and are ready to explore. They are stronger, bigger, and more coordinated. While some would scramble awkwardly up a couple stairs then panic, within a breath, they are now all apparently breaking through the pen and leaping up the stairs without any inhibitions.

Exhaustion

Have you ever had a puppy? At six weeks of age? Do you know how much energy they have? How much mess they make? Multiply that by seven.

Oh we love them. And given their enthusiasm, they love us. They are no longer content with staying in their pen in the basement with pumpkin mush kibble, they want to chase the brat pack, chew on computer cords, hide under the tables, and generally create chaos.

Oh it is fun. But it is exhausting. I now have two floors of the house that need to be scrubbed. Yes, the pups are doing awesome at paper training, but now and again there's a "miss." And let's not forget that newspaper is also a great toy. I try to keep up, but I have had to resign myself to the reality that no matter how many Clorox wipes I use, how much Lysol floor cleaner, the Shark steam cleaner, or anything, my house smells like a dog kennel.

Growing

It's exciting to see your babies grow and explore. As parents, we all revel in it. Until the babies start to get into things they shouldn't. The same thing goes for puppies – and in our case, x 7.

Once the pups figured out how to scale the barrier to the pen, there was no holding them back. I'm quite certain that, even if we had put in a bigger barrier, all that would happen is they would use each other as steps and haul the other ones over. So we gave up and simply puppy-proofed the basement and gave them room to roam.

Unfortunately, as it happened now and again, the basement door wouldn't be closed tight and would end up opened, often due to an overly curious schnauzer scratching at the door to be let in. The first sign this occurred was hearing said schnauzer racing up the steps then flying down the hallway. The second sign was what could only be described as a puppy stampede coming up those same steps and down the same hallway in hot pursuit.

While cute, it is also not good for young puppies, especially when dealing with larger breed dogs that can be prone to physical ailments such as hip dysplasia. In the early weeks of their lives, their bones and joints are growing quickly and prone to injury and potential deformity. Our instruction was to keep them from too much climbing and jumping – particularly jumping off things - as much as possible. This included climbing up and down stairs.

This was fine when they had first arrived as they lacked the size, strength, and coordination to even consider navigating the stairs. But once they grew and figured them out, they actually quite enjoyed the stairs. As we had a two-story house with a basement, this meant my home became a maze of baby gates blocking the stairwells. We were also extremely careful with them when we brought them up on the furniture for cuddles, never letting them jump down by themselves.

As the pups get bigger, they get closer to adoption, which means getting check by the vet and getting the first of their vaccinations.

Blog: V-litter goes to the Vet

Sarge took time off work to come with me to take the puppies to the vet for their first shots. But we had one problem: what do we do with Valley? Bringing her with us was the only solution, but we were concerned how she would react to this new experience.

Well, it was a little bit of an adventure trying to get her into the car (we have been so focused on puppies, we haven't been leash training her – oops!) but we did manage it. Step one done.

We got to the vet clinic and Sarge unloaded the puppies while I kept an eye on Valley, who had already snuck into the back hatch of the car. I tried to coax her out, but she wouldn't have anything to do with it. But just a little "c'mon, Valley" from her crush, Sarge, and she was jumping out, wagging her tail, and prepared to follow him anywhere.

Once in the vet's office, we started with the girls, with Vespa first on deck. She was hilarious. She wasn't impressed with any of it, especially not the thermometer. Next up – Vixen. Typical Vixen, barely flinched during the entire exam, didn't even seem to notice when she was vaccinated.

Finally, it was Violet's turn. True to form, she was the happy medium between lively Vespa and the sedate Vixen. She wasn't thrilled about going onto the scale, though (can't say I blame her …)

Time for the boys. Vlad, such a big, sweet cuddle, remained calm the entire time. After Vlad came Victor, the energetic gentleman.His ears can be rather expressive, as evidenced when it came time to take his temperature.

Time for Vanhalen. He is such a funny little guy. He can be so calm yet so playful and silly. He took everything like a trooper, but also seems a little self conscious about his weight, as he kept sneaking a foot off the scale.

Last – but definitely not least – was Vaughn, who was the biggest of the litter.The typical gentle giant he is, he barely fussed at all during the entire visit. Such a sweet guy.

So how did Valentina fare during all this? Exceptional. Within five minutes of being in the room, she was eating treats from the vet's hand, she laid on the floor resting albeit watchful of all going on.

As for us, well, it was warm in the room and trying to get wiggly puppies out of a kennel without the others getting out and causing all kinds of chaos wore us out. Thankfully the vaccinations tired the puppies out this evening because I needed the rest …

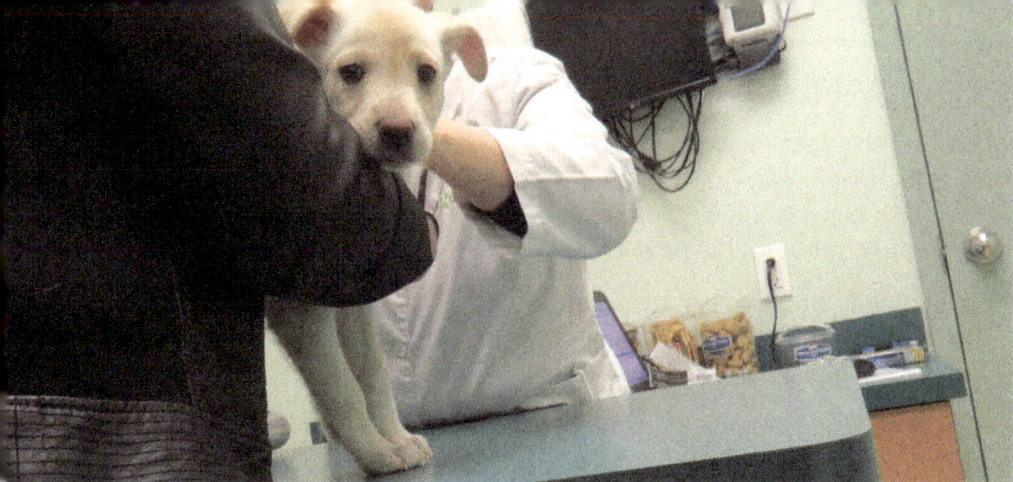

Veterinary Care

If you have pets and are planning to foster for a rescue, it is strongly recommended you ensure your pet's vaccinations are up-to-date. Many animals coming into a rescue are strays or abandoned, and their care history – including vaccinations – is unknown. Many rescues will have an animal examined by a veterinarian and vaccinated before ever being put into a foster care situation. However, emergency situations do arise, and the animal may need to be placed before seen by a veterinarian, so it is better to be safe than sorry. Puppies generally receive their first set of vaccinations at the tender age of eight weeks, as what happened with our foster litter.

Animal rescues usually have a network of veterinary clinics they work with and with whom they have made special arrangements, including reduced rates and payment plans. The rescue will often arrange the veterinary appointments themselves and either have you or another rescue volunteer take the foster to the appointment. Do not book an appointment yourself unless specifically directed to by the rescue as you can run the risk of the clinic not honouring the rates or even requiring you to pay the bill yourself.

I strongly encourage you attend the appointment if possible as the veterinarian may have questions about your foster that only you may be able to answer. Your presence can also help reduce stress for the animal, and help you understand more about the recommendations being made for his or her care.

Dogs, be they puppies or adults, generally handle vaccinations quite well, but the veterinarian will advise you of any adverse side effects that may require special care or even an emergency vet visit. Usually, the dog just ends up being quiet and sleepy for the day (yes, it was a welcome break!)

As prepared as you may be for a trip to the veterinarian, there is one treatment that defies preparation: deworming.

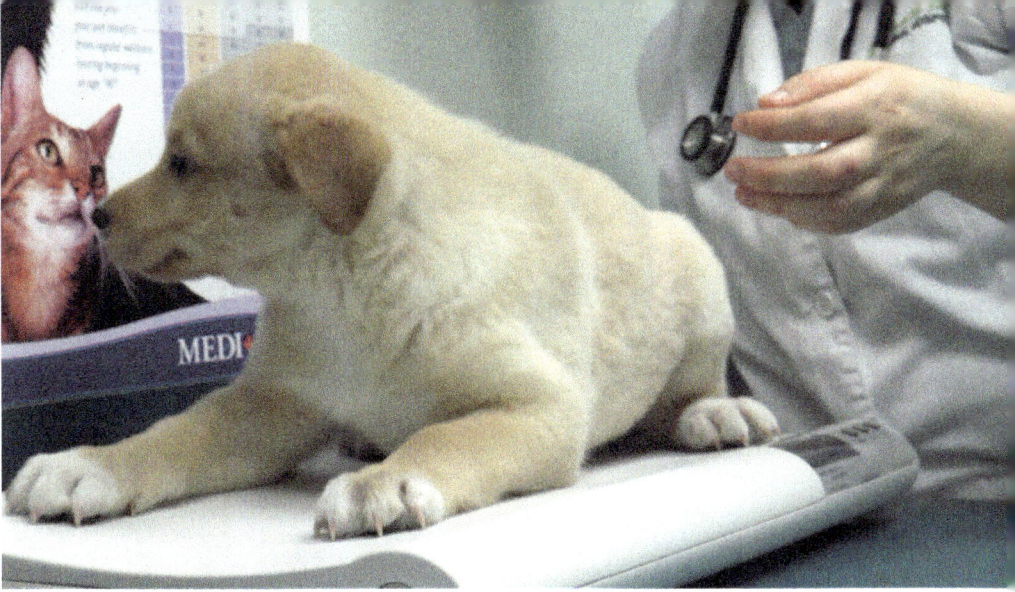

Blog: WORMS

The pups will be eight weeks on Monday, so we are getting them ready to go to their new homes. The vaccinations were Tuesday, so deworming was next. The rescue organizer dropped off the pills Friday night and Sarge and I took on the task of deworming.

I didn't realize giving them the pills was the easy part.

Now, I deworm my dogs regularly. But they do their business outside. And we have a long handled shovel and rake kit for picking up in the back yard. And nothing in my past prepared me for what I saw this morning.

With a v-litter open house today and tomorrow, we wanted to clean the house a bit so it doesn't look like we are always knee deep in puppy poop. Sarge worked on the upstairs – I headed down to clean the pen.

Sarge was happily cleaning away when I suddenly come up the stairs, gagging and retching. I can barely speak. I race to the sink, scared I'm going to vomit. All I am capable of getting out is "worms. omigawd worms." then gag and retch some more. Sarge's turn to laugh.

When I first went to pick up the newspaper, I saw things looked a little different. As I got closer, I saw something unusual. I wondered "when did they eat spaghetti? Or rice?"

Then I realized what it was. Worms.

Lots of worms. Everywhere I looked, there were worms.

I will not be eating spaghetti - or rice - for a long, long time …

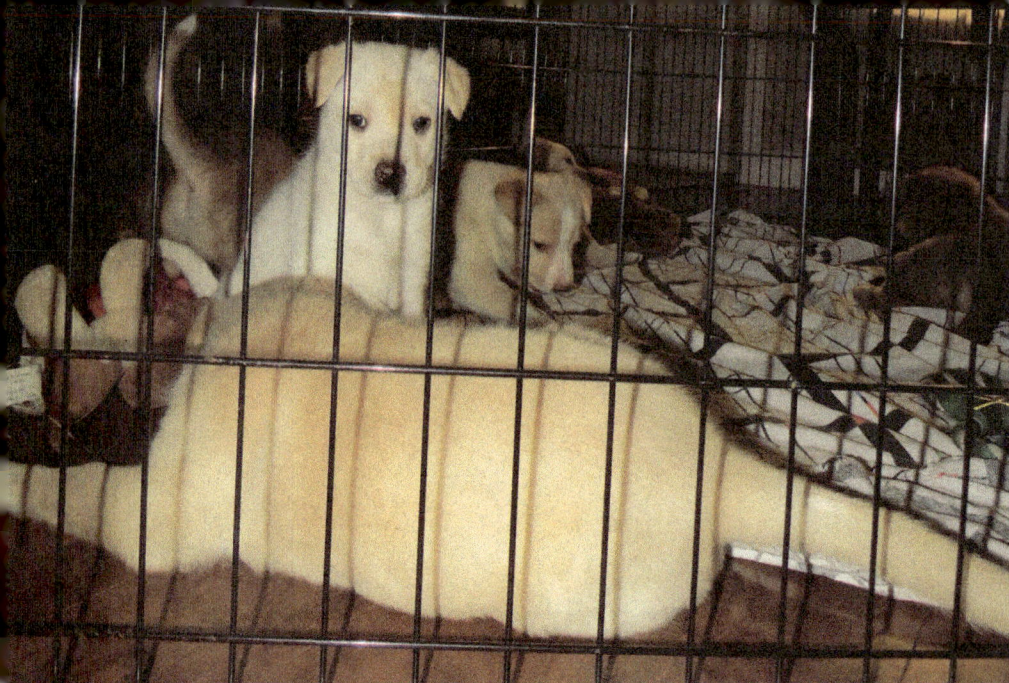

Preparing for Adoption
Sleeping arrangements, housebreaking, and training

Sleeping arrangements

Once the puppies were old enough to eat kibble and basically weaned from Valley, she started sleeping in the room with us. Maybe not an ideal situation, particularly from a training perspective, but all our other dogs slept with us, so it was just instinctive for us to include her.

In retrospect, it would have been wiser to set up a separate kennel space for her and let her get accustomed to sleeping in there by herself to help with transitioning her to her new home. They bought her a kennel she use during the day for naps and such, but her first night was a tough one for her and her adoptive mom, both of whom slept by the door as Valley waited for us to come back to get her. (I'll hang on while you get a tissue.)

As noted before, we don't have issues with dog kennels and use them for our own dogs; however, Valentina wasn't our dog. It is always a good idea to follow the recommendations of the rescue and adhere to their preferences as, ultimately, it will make the transition much easier for the adoptive family.

Separating the mother from the puppies was a normal, logical step. But separating the puppies from each other at night was a new premise for me.

Blog: Blondes vs. Brunettes Part I

The puppies are now just shy of five weeks old, meaning they are maybe three weeks away from going into their new fur-ever homes. Therefore, we have started the process of getting them used to being on their own a little more.

Step 1: Bring them upstairs to socialize with the brat pack.

Status: Achieved. However, the brat pack is pretty much terrified of the little barky things with the sharp teeth that love to chase tails and attack schnauzer beards. Valley just lays around watching the chaos. I'm pretty sure she's laughing inside as the pups are now terrorizing someone other than her …

Step 2: Start separating the pups into groups and have them spend the night away from Valentina.

Status: Process started. We borrowed a smaller pen that we brought upstairs to contain the pups while they played and got exposed to a new environment. They settled quickly, even had a nap.

When it came time for bed, I had to decide not only how I was going to separate them, but also keep track of who stayed up and who went downstairs.

That's where the Blondes vs. the Brunettes came in: I thought separating by colour the first time would be the easiest. But who would stay away from their mom first?

Truth be told, I had no idea WHAT was going to happen regardless of who was kept away from her. So I started with the brunettes.

Step 3: Set up sleeping area.

Status: Complete. I put a kennel inside the temporary pen, door open, for them to move as they saw fit.

Step 4: Go to bed and get some sleep.

Status: Surprisingly enough – SUCCESS! Blondes vs. Brunettes Night 1 worked out very well! The three settled down quickly and I didn't hear a peep from them until the regular 2:30 a.m.-let-the-brat-pack-out consitutional. Even then, they were just curious about what was going on. I let Valley out to do her thing, and then decided to take the three downstairs for the rest of the night, just in case.

Tonight, it will be the Blondes' turn … thankfully, I don't have to work tomorrow … just in case …

I listened with rapt attention to the instructions on how to separate the pups into small groups to help them get accustomed to sleeping apart from the rest of the litter.

I would like to say that I would consciously choose a more confident pup to be with one less so. Or that I did it according to who was already selected for adoption and needed to be prepared to sleep on his or her own sooner than later. Truth be told, there was no rhyme nor reason behind my selection of pups to segregate at any time other than by colour so I could keep track.

I broke the groups down into smaller sections until eventually it was only two in the upstairs kennel. And when I knew that an adopted pup was scheduled to be picked up in a couple days, I would also separate him or her to sleep alone, hoping that it would make the first few nights in their new home easier. I didn't hear from all the adoptive parents as to whether this strategy worked or not, but I do know that VanHalen and Vixen were less than happy about being in a strange new place on their own. But they did adapt to their new homes very quickly, with minimal accidents, thanks to our housebreaking skills.

Housebreaking

Living in town, I got the weekly local newspaper, plus numerous flyers throughout the week. I recycled, which mean that I usually had a few weeks' of newspapers stashed away waiting to go to the recycling depot.

That supply vanished quite quickly, and soon I was raiding the recycle bins at work for tossed newspapers. Not surprising when you are swapping out approximately 250 square feet of newspaper from the basement floor at least twice a day. And that was before we started bringing the pups upstairs.

So it was, indeed, a relief, when the puppies started recognizing patches of newspaper rather than the floor as the place to mark their spot.

Blog: Newspaper - not just for reading

I think the puppies are becoming paper-trained. O.o

Faithful readers of the blog have heard my complaints of being knee-deep in puppy poop, dodging puppy landmines, and having wall-to-wall newspaper in my basement. Oh, and let's not forget the dramatic increase in my garbage output as I dispose of used newspaper.

Well, the other night when I had the pups upstairs for a socialization time, I noticed them looking around for a place to do their business, so I quickly put down some newspaper. A couple of the pups headed straight for the paper to relieve themselves.

Interesting.

On Sunday, with my rubber boots on to protect my ankles, I went about cleaning up the puppy pen. As I picked up all the paper, I noticed they were starting to go to one spot. Out of curiosity, I decided to only put paper in that part of the pen.

Later that evening, the pups were once again upstairs for socialization time. Some paper was put on the floor away from the upstairs overnight pen. Again, pups started heading for the paper to relieve themselves.

This is getting good.

This morning, I went downstairs to feed the hungry babies and lo and behold, with the exception of one little puppy pile, all other mess was on the newspaper in the one section of the pen.

With only one-third of the pen covered in paper, it was nothing at all for me to clear out the old and lay down fresh paper. While in the process, Vaughn was looking around, and I quickly put some down for him. He went to the freshly-laid paper and peed right in the middle of it.

I was so happy I could have cried.

Vanhalen was next, and although I thought he was just going in the general area (where no paper was down yet as I was still in the middle of cleaning), once he moved, I saw he had actually managed to position himself right over a left-over piece of paper that hadn't been cleaned yet. He completely missed the floor. Vlad quickly followed suit.

I find it amusing that it was the girls who seemed to be more confident and curious, but it is the boys who seem to pick up on paper-training quicker, although, as evidenced by the mess being contained in one area, they are all catching on.

They really are growing up fast … *sniff*

Suffice it to say that newspaper covered in puppy poop does not go into the recycle bin, and had to be thrown in the garbage. In my community, as with others, we have a limit on the amount of garbage that can be picked up each week (only what can fit in our supplied bin). As a result, I had a number of bags stashed away until my level of garbage returned to normal. Not ideal, but necessary.

At the same time we had Valley and her pups, there was another foster with a mother dog and her litter of pups, all about the same age. We were provided with much of the same supplies, including blankets and towels, Lysol disinfecting wipes, and a package of puppy pads. While the other foster continued using the pads, I personally don't like them as much simply from an environmental perspective – plus they're very expensive. To protect the floors in the basement, we laid down thick rubber mats and put the newspaper over top. This also had the added bonus of providing a bit more spring for bouncing puppies, protecting their joints.

When it comes to actually housetraining, there are thousands of "experts," all with their opinions and sure-fire methods of housebreaking dogs, whether they are puppies or adults. Whatever methodology your rescue prefers or recommends, the basics are quite simple.

As mentioned previously, kennels go a long way in helping to housebreak dogs as they generally do not like messing in their den. Establish a routine, including letting them out of their kennel and immediately outside first thing in the morning and after being locked up for any period of time, and praising for doing their business outside.

Note dogs will need to go outside again as early as twenty minutes to an hour after eating, and even sooner if you notice he or she has just taken in a big drink of water. Keep this in mind, watch for the signs, and reward the dog by letting it do its business outside.

Another trick is to keep them close to you by keeping them on the leash even when in the house. That way, you will know right away if the dog is about to make a mess, and you can quickly correct by taking him or her outside.

Note: correction does NOT include yelling at the dog, hitting or otherwise striking the dog, or rubbing the dog's nose in its mess. Those antiquated measures do little to build trust and are ineffective.

If it is an adult that keeps messing in the house, you will need to work with the rescue – and possibly a veterinarian and a dog trainer – to rule out medical or behavioural issues and work out an appropriate strategy.

It's a bit of a different story for puppies. According to some experts, it isn't until a dog is between 12 and 16 weeks old before it will have sufficient control of the bladder and bowels to be properly housebroken. Even then, it can't be expected they will be able to hold anything in for much more than a couple of hours. Being aware of this will help manage expectations and help reduce frustrations.

At a certain age, it becomes instinctive even for puppies not to mess where they sleep, and I watched this happen with my little foster pack. Once they got old enough and were familiar with the outdoors, they extended their reach to wanting to go outside to do their business.

The suggestions for training adults holds true for pups – kennels, routine, and keeping them close. Sharing your routine with the adoptive family will help them build on the foundation you've started and make for a happy and successful adoption.

Unfortunately, with several pups in the house, it was nearly impossible for me to have a proper training regime. That said, a number of the pups were adopted out at eight weeks, and the housebreaking – and most of the training - more logically fell upon the adoptive family.

Training

Four years later, as I read through my old blog posts and reflect on that crazy time in my life, I am not quite certain who trained whom. If I am honest with myself and with you, I would confess that it was the dogs who trained me.

Blog: What's in a Name?

The day Valley and the pups arrived was the day that Vixen was given her name. Being the only black dog in the group, and a female, it was promptly decided that Vixen should be her name.

I wasn't sure of the choice. Vixen is the smallest of the litter, dainty, petite, and seemed a bit timid. She didn't seem like a Vixen. Yeah. Right.

She had me fooled at first. When it was pumpkin mush feeding time, she would hang back from the group, crying pathetically, seeming too small and delicate to fight her way into fray to get a couple of bites. The same occurred when it was time to nurse off Valley. Such a sad, small, little girl.

So, tenderheart that I am, I gave Vixen some extra care and attention.

At feeding time, she would receive her own special dish of pumpkin mush, separate from the crowd so she wouldn't have to compete with the others. We would do whatever it takes to ensure this fragile little creature survives …

Now it is debatable. Did the special treatment allow her to build up strength to be more competitive with her six siblings. Or was she playing me?

Vixen is a vixen. She will play the "I'm just a tiny little girl" card, and then pounce. She will cry when her bigger brothers wrestle with her, but once free, she will attack and give them a good chomp. She will sit back and give a grin, letting us know that she isn't the timid, delicate little girl we once thought. In fact, she, along with her two sisters, Vespa and Violet, seem to hold their own pretty darn good with those four brothers.

I should have known better. She was the first of the group to adopt a toy, a stuffed baby big bird, with whom she cuddles – when she isn't chewing on his face. The puppy adventure continues …

29

What you are capable of doing when it comes to training puppies is quite limited for the first few weeks of their life. For the most part, it is trying to discourage them from biting ankles, toes, and other dogs, from chewing on furniture, electrical cords, and other dogs (yes, this was intentional), and that kennels are a good place to sleep.

Had we known that our two week adventure would extend so much longer, and that we would have older pups in our care, we likely would have done more research on training. Or delayed our home renovations so we could have spent more time training. How cute would it have been to have Victor and Vespa sitting on command, giving high-fives, doing a perfect heel, and more during the meet and greets? No regrets, though. Had that happened, they may have been adopted sooner and not have ended up with the wonderful couple who have given them the perfect home.

Valentina was a different story, and much of her life with us was training her to be a pet. Okay, it was less training, and more spoiling, but you get the picture. From helping her navigate stairs, taking car rides, and how to behave on a leash, it was up to us to provide the basics to our dear Valentina.

One thing that has to be said about rescue dogs – and many, many others have reported this as well – is they seem to understand you are giving them a second chance at life and they are extremely grateful and will do anything to please you. Valentina was the epitome of this, which still is extraordinary to me given the life she had before she came into the rescue.

If you have any questions or concerns regarding training, connect with your rescue. Some have even partnered with trainers, who will come and help you with specific training issues. If this resource is available to you, definitely take advantage of it.

Blog: Adventures of Valentina

As stated before, the puppies have consumed our lives. So much, we neglected the all-important Valentina. And when I say neglect, I don't mean we have ignored her or anything. I mean in the context of readying her for her new life in a new home with a new family, specifically by not working on having her on a leash.

If you have ever put a leash on a dog that never had one, you would already know that they will stop dead if you attempt to pull them. Hence, why we put the leash on her yesterday and just let her walk around and get used to the feeling of it.

The brat pack was getting ansy so I figured I would take them to the off leash park. But what do I do with Valley? Take her or leave her?

Yes, I was nervous, but she had never let me down before, so I thought I would give it a go – let's bring Valley as well.

I grabbed Valley's leash and she followed me down the steps to the car. With the others already in, she was a little hesitant about jumping in, so I had to give her a lift to coax her into my car.

At the park, we had a couple of initial moments when she wasn't quite sure what was going on and she would stop and lay down. A little coaxing and encouragement and she was soon tagging along beautifully. She would switch from side to side but eventually we found our rhythm and you would hardly know there was a dog on the other end of the leash.

She watched while the others ran around and she would try to go but once she got to the end of the leash she would stop and look at me and drop back to a walk.

The whole thing was going extremely well. The park was quiet, very few people out to So, while in the back side of the park where no one else was, I decided to give her a couple minutes of freedom. I let her loose, then crouched down and called her back. She immediately returned to me.

I let her go play for a couple minutes, called her back again. Second time was a little slower to respond as she was very intrigued with a smell she found, but she came back, tail wagging, big smile on her face. Her recall was really quite extraordinary.

For nine or so weeks, her life was contained within the walls of human habitation, but she never seemed anxious about her containment. And while experiencing the outdoors at the park, she was also enjoying being with her "pack," even if they are a bunch of brats.

31

5 Social Training - not just for the dogs

Social media, Photos, photos and more photos, and showcasing personality

Social Media

Chances are you are on some form of social media, be it Facebook, Twitter, Instagram, Snapchat, or whatever. Chances are, if you are a lover of animals, you are following at least one (likely more) animal rescues on social media, most likely Facebook. Chances are, it is through social media - most likely Facebook - that you became interested in fostering for an animal rescue.

Whatever your comfort level is in social media, if you are fostering for a rescue, there will likely be a push for you to help promote the rescue and its adoptive animals on your social media channels.

If you did your research in Chapter 1, then you've already determined this is an organization to which you want to be associated, so it shouldn't be a problem. And, as you'll note throughout this book, social media can be a great opportunity to connect with people who adopt the animals you have fostered, which can be a very rewarding experience.

Social media can also help you connect with rescue volunteers and other fosters, which can be a great support network and source of information and resources. And, for Terry and me, it became a way to create and continue friendships with other volunteers and adoptive families.

You will also likely be asked to contribute content to be shared on the rescue's social media channels. Luckily for you, many rescues will have someone that coordinates their social media on their behalf so you don't have to worry about being plugged into their page. But you will need to connect with this person as it is likely this individual who will be posting all the photos and stories about your foster. Rescues usuallly have a process for all of this, so be sure to ask what it is and what supports might be available to you, just in case you aren't as technologically-savvy as you would like to be.

As I mentioned earlier, in addition to sharing photos with the rescue for its Facebook page, I chose to write a blog as a different way to showcase my foster family. As a writer, it was instinctive for me to do it this way. It allowed me to post when I wanted to, share photos along with stories, and provide insight into fostering as well as sharing information on the dogs. I shared the link to each blog post with the rescue social media coordinator, who then shared the

link via Facebook for all their followers to read. It proved to be quite successful. In fact, there was another mother dog and her pups who were about the same age as my crew that were not being adopted as quickly simply because people were connecting with the stories and the photos in my blog. Oops.

Facebook is definitely the go-to social media of choice - but don't limit yourself, especially with so many options, like Instagram and Snapchat, where the focus is the photos. And speaking of photos ...

Blog: We be fabulous ...

Sunday was an exciting day for the V-family as they were invited to show off their fabulousness as part of the pet photography training session hosted by Chelsea and Teann. (P.S. I arrived in time to see the tail end – no pun intended – of the course and it looked awesome. I wish I could have taken in the whole thing!)

The adventure started when we tried to get out the door.

First, Vespa and Victor, despite being the smaller of the litter, are still too big to travel in the kennel in which all seven pups first arrived (what does that tell you!!!) That said, they do like to squeeze in there in the evenings when they want to nap. So, I had to grab the larger – and heavier – kennel and put within it the two squirmy excited pups.

Second, anytime the brat pack sees a leash, they automatically assume that it is time to go for a walk or to the off-leash park, even if the leash is only put on one dog – in this situation, Valley. Anytime I tried to get Valley out the door, the brat pack tried to squeeze out as well. Any attempt to reprimand caused Valley to back off. Finally, I just chased all of them out into the back yard and snuck out with Valentina and the puppies.

Valentina is awesome at car rides. It did take a little bit to get her in the car at first, but she settled into the passenger seat and enjoyed the ride.

The puppies … not so much. They were rather expressive with their dismay, but I can't really blame them. Their first car ride involved needles and a thermometer in an "exit-only" area. Thankfully, they settled down and were quiet for most of the 40 minute drive.

I understood that Valley, Vespa and Victor were going to be models for the students. I did not understand that I was also going to be part of the photo shoot. I am grateful I opted to wear jeans and my nice sandals rather than my usual weekend attire of sweatpants and my chewed up kennel-cleaning sandals …

I had already come to realize that Valley looked to Sarge and I as pack leaders; I didn't realize until Sunday the extent of the attachment between me, her, and the pups. To help get some photos, I was interacting with Valley and the puppies, running around, calling them back from their explorations of the arena. And this is how I ended up in the photos.

I do have to thank Chelsea of Vitality Images for taking some great shots of the dogs. As an out of shape runner, I am not crazy about getting my picture taken right now, but I can actually live with these ones (although I would be okay with some photoshopping …)

Photos, photos and more photos

You know the saying - a picture says a thousand words. The glimmer in the eye, a big toothy smile, a playful pose, it all captures the heart of a potential adopter and it is your job as a foster to capture personality in photos.

Some rescues have a professional photographer they work with to get those magazine-worthy images that everyone loves. Don't worry - you don't need to compete. However, you may be asked to have the photographer come over to take photos or for you to take your foster someplace to be photographed. A word of advice: dress as though you'll be in the photos, because you just might end up in a few whether you realize it or not.

If you have an actual digital camera - not just your smartphone - I recommend pulling it out and learning how to use it. First, it will save space on your device, and second, a camera used properly can capture some images that you simply can't reproduce on a phone. Especially action shots. And you can't just post pictures of sleeping dogs. If you aren't sure how to use your camera, introductory photography courses are reasonably inexpensive and a lot of fun. I wish I had taken lessons prior to fostering (this is my disclaimer as to the photographic quality of my own photos).

Of course, the ideal is to supplement the camera with a smartphone, especially to get those hilarious moments shared quickly on social media. I can't even imagine what my foster experience would have been if Snapchat or Instagram was around way back then and I was able to add captions to some of those ridiculously cute and silly puppy moments.

Which brings me to my next point: while it is true a picture is worth a thousand words, sometimes the picture isn't enough to tell the story.

Blog: Life according to Vespa

6:00 a.m. Zzzzzzzzzzzzzzzzzzzzzzzzzzz ... what's that? The dog next door is awake and outside. Oh no. Must pee. Time to wake up my brother – he barks much louder than me. That'll wake up the humans.

6:15 a.m. How did I end up back in my kennel so quick? *Sigh* Oh well. I guess I can snooze for another hour. Zzzzzzzzzzzzzzzzzzzzzzzzzz

7:15 a.m. I hear the humans. They're awake. Time for breakfast!

7:55 a.m. Human tries to get me to go into my kennel. I'm too smart for that. I'll come running right up to it but I won't go in. Wait. Is that a treat? Oh I love treats! Oh no! Human picking me up and putting me in the kennel! Oh well, I'll snuggle up with Victor and have a nap. Zzzzzzzzzzzzzzzzzzzz

12:05 p.m. Yay! The momma human is home! Must be lunchtime! What do I do first? Pee? Eat? Drink some water? OH HECK NO – I see the schnauzer! Must chew on schnauzer beard! And then give kisses to all the big dogs! Oh life is so much fun!

12:25 p.m. Seriously? Back in the kennel? Oh well, my tummy is full from lunch, so I'll have another nap. Zzzzzzzzzzzzzzzzzzzzzzzzzz

4:35 p.m. Yay! The humans are back! Time to play play play! I can run inside and run outside and run back inside and chew on the schnauzer then go wrestle with Victor, then I grab a squeaky toy! Oh I love squeaky toys! Oops. Time to smell the whole backyard to make sure no one snuck in while I was napping. Are we going to the park today? I like the park. I'm hungry! I'm thirsty! Potty break! Yay more big dogs to chase. I need to lay down for a rest. Ok, naptime done, I want to play with the humans! Oooooooh. They picked me up and I get to cuddle on a lap. I like that. I will reward them with my happy little puppy kisses. Ooh schnauzer! Must chase! What's that? I'll chase it! Ouch! Why did that hurt? Oooh there it goes again – wait, Victor, no! I think that's my tail! Don't bite so hard. Oh I'm thirsty again. I think I'll lay down right here. What's that? ooooh I'm going to gnaw on this for a while ... hmmm ... tastes like foot ...

(this goes on over and over and over until ...)

9:30 p.m. Zzzzzzzzzzzzzzzzzzzzzzzzzzzzzzzzzzzz

2:30 a.m. I hear something ... what is it? It sounds like "tick tick tick tick" right above me. Is that the big dogs awake? I'll just go back to sleep. Wait. It sounds like a herd of elephants coming down the stairs. Yay it's the big dogs! Let me out, I want to play with them.

2:40 a.m. Zzzzzzzzzzzzzzzzzzzzzzzzzzzzzzzzzzzzz

Showcasing Personalities

Successful adoptions happen when the right pet is matched with the right family. It's easy enough to ask people about their lifestyle and what qualities and characteristics they want in a dog, but you can't ask the dog to describe itself to be matched with the right person. As a foster, you get to be the observer, learn about the dog's traits and personality, and help tell his or her story.

Don't worry - you don't need to be a professional writer to do this.

All it takes is spending some time observing and getting to know the dog. Or, in my case, dogs.

Generally, puppies love cuddle time, but Vespa would only tolerate it for so long and then she wanted down to explore. She was adventurous, fearless, and basically the going concern. Unlike Victor, who was content to cuddle for hours. Vixen liked to go off on her own away from the rest of the litter, while Vlad could usually be found snuggled up to his mom. Valley was independent, but loved being with people and would do anything to please you.

Once you start seeing their personalities and recognizing those traits, your strategy then becomes capturing those moments in words and in photos. For me, it was my blog. But even if you're sharing photos with the rescue to post on Facebook, include a quick little story about what was happening that would give insight to the dog's personality.

For example, I managed to get a quick picture of Vespa climbing over the board we put up to try and keep all the puppies in the pen. In sharing the photo, I could say: "My second attempt at containing Miss Vespa has failed! It's going to take some more wit on my part to contain this curious and agile puppy. But wow, she has the makings of an agility champion!"

So not only is it a cute picture of a puppy climbing, but now you have an idea that this puppy is pretty smart and physically active - which is awesome if that is what I'm looking for in a dog, which may prompt me to contact the rescue to arrange a meet and greet.

Blog: SWM looking for his true love

My name is Victor and I am almost 11 weeks old. My hobbies including chasing my sister Vespa, biting schnauzer beards, chewing on bones, and exploring the great outdoors (a.k.a. the backyard).

I'm a natural blonde and am told I have the most handsome and soulful set of eyes. I like to play but have good manners (no matter what my current roommates have to say).

I am kennel trained and housebroken. I can sleep through the night – unless my sister wakes me – but I will go back to sleep after a late night "constitutional."

Nothing makes me happier than to make you happy. When I'm a bit bigger, I'll enjoy walks along the beach, picnics in the dog park, and sleeping on a pillow at the foot of your bed.

Not sure why a handsome guy like me hasn't been snapped up yet, but I'm hoping my soul-mate will find me soon. If you think I'm the guy for you, put in your application today.

Kisses and tail-wags, Victor

6 Meet and Greets
Preparing your home, your foster family, and yourself

I don't think I said the words "my house doesn't always look like this" more often than I did during the time Valentina and her puppies lived with us. My normally clean and organized home became a two-level dog kennel, with newspaper as the primary floor covering.

It wasn't too bad in the early weeks. The puppies were small enough that I could keep them down in the basement except for when we were specifically bringing them up to socialize. That helped keep the main floor clean, and I only needed to focus my efforts on the basement. As they got older and wanted to be on the main floor with us, the mess grew along with them and I finally had to resolve myself to the fact that my house looked - and smelled – like a dog kennel.

Thankfully, those who came to the house for meet and greets were understanding and forgiving (at least they seemed to be). I tried to make myself feel better by believing visitors were more interested in the pups than my housekeeping skills.

Blog: How many feet are in your house?

That was a question my sister asked when I told her I currently have twelve dogs in my home. Let it be known she isn't very good at math

I will be getting rather up close and personal with 28 of those feet as I start clipping the toenails on each one as they, like the baby teeth, are getting rather sharp and long, as evidenced by the scratches on my chest from attempting puppy cuddles.

Oh, puppy cuddles. How they have changed in the last week! I have officially had Valentina and her seven babies for 9 days and they are GROWING! A week ago, it was easy to grab two of them and just cuddle and snuggle. They will now put up with it for about five minutes and then it is time to investigate.

Well, there are some exceptions. The boys mostly. Vanhalen is probably the cuddliest of them all, and it doesn't matter if it is with momma, his siblings, or people – he just likes to cuddle.

Vlad, on the other hand, is a total momma's boy. Ironic that he is the biggest of the litter and yet the biggest suck. Oh but he is so handsome.

I like to refer to Vlad and Violet as twins, with her the more independent one. They have a beautiful sable coat, their mother's beautiful temperament, and are wonderful dogs. I think Violet found her perfect home as her new momma spent the entire afternoon snuggling with her yesterday and she was in her glory.

The puppy meet-and-greets are going to be an interesting phase in my puppy foster experience. I am looking forward to meeting the prospective families for the puppies and Valentina, but I am also finding myself a protective mom – I want to be sure all eight go to their perfect homes where they will be loved as much as I love them. So far, so good.

Also, for the first time ever, I am actually going to exceed the limit for garbage disposal, all because of the sheer volume of newspaper I spread out – and pick up – on a daily basis.

I'm still knee deep in puppy poop, but I'm still smiling.

Preparing your Home

Without a doubt, it is important to have some semblance of clean when you are expecting company. While newspaper with fresh piles and wet spots suggests the pups are at least paper trained, it also signals they are still messing in the house. The intent is not to lie to prospective adopters, but rather show the care and attention you are giving the pups by keeping the space tidy.

In truth, most of the meet and greets occurred before the pups were at the adoptable age of eight weeks and it would be completely unrealistic to expect them to be housebroken at that age. Still, less puppy poop, better meet and greet.

One requirement of the rescue was that all visitors use hand sanitizer before picking up any of the puppies. I wasn't sure why, except perhaps the potential for bringing in something that might harm the pups before they had been vaccinated. If anything, the hand sanitizer was ready and available for after the visitors were done handling the pups, as was the bathroom in case they preferred soap and water.

Aside from that, try to keep the meet and greet space as tidy, warm and inviting as possible (no, drinks and snacks are not necessary or required). You are showcasing a potential family pet, and whatever you can do to help create that vision of the pet living in their home will help with the adoption.

Blog: Bathing babies

As can be expected, the puppies have gotten a little "messy." I can only say it is because of their youthful puppy antics that take place anywhere … no matter what is on the floor …

And before anyone makes any comments about the condition of the floor, please know that I clean up at least twice a day after the puppies. They just poop so much!!!

So how does one bath seven puppies?

Idea 1: Put them all in the bathtub.

Idea 2: Wash them one at a time in the kitchen sink.

As tempting as the bathtub was, I envisioned seven squirmy, unhappy puppies splashing around in the tub, trying to get out, and soaking everything but still managing to come out unwashed.

Kitchen sink it was.

So I recruited Sarge fresh out of the shower (sucker) and we started the puppy-wash assembly line. I filled sink one with soapy water, sink two with clean water, and started the puppy torture.

I washed. Sarge dried. I wish I had pictures, but I was not about to subject our camera to that level of torture.

We started with Vespa. Oh, sweet, feisty little Vespa. She did not enjoy the bath at all. Maggie was no better. Actually Vixen didn't enjoy it too much either. Seems weird that none of the girls liked getting a bath.

The boys varied, but the one who enjoyed it the most was Vanhalen! Oh he is such a sweet little guy, so calm, so trusting.

Once bathed, all puppies went into the upstairs pen to relax, dry off, and socialize as appropriate.

But it wasn't supposed to just be bathtime, but also Blondes vs. Brunettes Part 2 of Separate Sleeping. So what happened?

By the time we were ready for bed, all pups were calm, relaxed, and sleeping. It just seemed wrong to wake them only to upset them (I really need "sucker" tattooed on my forehead). So, in keeping with the overall theme of separating pups from momma, we left the group upstairs on their own inside the pen.

Preparing your foster

The most important thing above all else is ensuring your foster looks his/her best. Whether that means a bath, a brush, a bandana around the neck, you get to show off how well this lovely creature has done under your care. Quite simply, if your foster doesn't look good, you don't look good. Okay, there are some circumstances that will be out of your control – like white puppies that insist on playing around in their orange pumpkin-mush poop right before visitors arrive - but for the most part, even a lick and a promise can go a long way (please don't literally lick the puppies)..

It's likely you have a routine in your household for the animals under your care, including your own and your foster. This includes meal times, exercise time, and nap time – for the dogs, not just you. Disrupting this schedule too much can make for some unhappy pets and an unpleasant meet and greet experience.

Work with your rescue to establish the most appropriate times to have meet and greets. For example, if you get home from work at 5 p.m., let the dogs out to do their business, then feed them right away, chances are they will need to go outside again within 20 minutes to an hour. This is important, especially for housebreaking a dog. The last thing you need is a disruption to your routine that will divert attention from the dog trying to give you cues that it needs to go outside and instead having an accident in the house.

Having a mom and a litter of pups also creates its own set of preparation. Depending on how protective the mom is, you may need to have her separated from the pups to avoid any incidents. But if she is as laid back as Valley was, that won't be a problem. Having a mom with a great temperament can be a great indicator of how the pups may turn out. It never hurts to check with the rescue as to what their preference would be.

Showing the puppies as a group can be highly entertaining for the visitor because, really, there are few things in this world cuter than young pups bouncing around and playing with each other. However, it can be quite distracting for the potential adopters, and suddenly it is less about assessing a puppy for adoption and more about having fun playing with puppies. And the visit ends up taking much longer than necessary. This is not what you want.

My strategy was simple. The application usually requires the person to indicate which pup they are interested in adopting. I would find out this information, and have that pup segregated – with or without Valentina - from the rest for the meet and greet. We would do the meet and greet upstairs rather than in the basement so they had one-on-one time with the dog to get to know the personality. With all the questions answered and all the hugs and snuggles completed, we would take the pup downstairs to be with the rest of the group and wrap up the visit.

We also tried our best to keep our dogs out of the way as well, and would lock them upstairs, or one of us would take them to the off leash park during the visit. There were times, of course, when this wasn't possible or, because of my blog, people wanted to meet the brat pack as well. Usually someone would fall in love with our lab cross, Cosmo, and want to adopt him, to which we would respond no, but the puppies all spend lots of time with him and he's been a good influence.

43

Blog: And then there were four ...

Tonight we said goodbye to little Miss Violet as she went home with her new family, including a brother named Pickles, who was also adopted from the same rescue.

I figured I had this routine down, but when it came time to say goodbye, I immediately started tearing up and had to try real hard to keep it together after she left with her new family. Oh but they are really nice people and Pickles certainly looks like he's done well, so I'm sure Violet will have a good life too. She is a precocious little one, perhaps even more so than Vespa – Violet's just sneakier about it …

I'm inclined to blame my tears on the lack of sleep. I'm hard pressed to blame the pups for the midnight wake up as it was actually Valentina, sleeping in our room, who decided she wanted downstairs for a snack, which of course woke the puppies. Then they woke up at 1 … then 2 … and 4:30 … but did actually sleep until almost 7. When I read the updates on little Vanhalen and hear how he's sleeping through the night, I will admit to being rather jealous. Mind you, he doesn't have four other littermates with him to disrupt his sleep …

I also received confirmation today that the homecheck for the family interested in Vaughn went great and he will be going home to a new family (including a kitty!) on Thursday. He has really changed in the last bit and proving himself to be a rather handsome guy, just the way he holds his head and carries himself.

Vlad's homecheck is also scheduled for this week, possibly Wednesday, so we will know soon if he has found himself his own home.

By the weekend, it could very well just be Valley, Victor, and Vespa, three of my favourites and yet no adoptions pending. And that surprises me to no end.

Another thing to prepare for is the family with a dog already looking to bring home a friend.

This dynamic requires a different strategy. Dogs can be quite protective of their homes and may see a visitor as a threat – whether it is someone coming to your home, or you taking the foster to a prospective family's home. The best situation is to find neutral territory to introduce the dogs to each other, particularly if they are both older.

 To make life easier, when the pups were older, we would do introductions in a local park or even the off leash park. When they were younger, this wasn't possible, so we would just do introductions in the front yard of our house, with Valentina and the rest inside. Easy peasy.

Okay - your house and your foster are ready – are you?

Blog: At least someone likes the snow

It's been rather busy around here, with adoptive family visits and meet and greets. Violet had lots of time with her new family on Saturday, and the pups were exhausted and crashed afterwards.

Sunday afternoon had two families coming to look at the puppies, with Victor and Vlad stealing the show and possibly some hearts. Time will tell the outcome of the visits. As usual, the pups were their quiet, charming selves, but the rescue coordinator stuck around long enough to see that, indeed, they are playful and rambunctious. Seriously, look at the state of my home and you can tell how energetic they are!

But I am grateful that they have their mother's temperament and are more curious than anything. Although Vespa is staring to think her name is "Vespa-no" as that is usually how her name is said … oh but she is such a sweetheart.

After everyone left, I saw the pups staring out the patio door … the sun was shining, the deck was warm, and much of the snow had melted off. Since they have already been trying to sneak out the patio doors anyway, I thought I'd let them spend some time outside and check things out. I let my camera tell the rest of the story.

Preparing yourself

This part was probably the most difficult for me given that I am actually an introvert. My home is my sanctuary and I don't usually like strangers coming through, espeically on a regular basis. Thankfully, I do okay when the focus isn't on me. I mean, really, all eyes were on Valentina and her pups, not me.

Introvert or extrovert, there are things you need to do to prepare. In the best-case scenario, a representative of the rescue will be there with you during the meet and greet to answer all the rescue-related questions. However, things happen, and you may find yourself flying solo or, if the family has your contact information, they may call you for follow-up questions. Defer to the rescue when you can, but it doesn't hurt to know the answers as well.

Know as much about the animal as possible, including age, type of food, habits, and personality. Even with a rescue representative there, as the animal has been living with you, you are the better person to answer those questions and the rescue will likely look to you to respond.

People will often ask about the breed. This is a tough question to answer unless your foster has documented information confirming the breed. More often than not, dogs are brought into care from animal shelters or found as strays. While there may be clues as to the breed, it is difficult to know for sure. Some people will ask simply because they may have fears or preconceived ideas about certain breeds (particularly those in the pitbull category) and will want some form of assurance that the dog is not one of those breeds. Be prepared to address these questions carefully and tactfully without attempting to mislead a potential adopter.

Be familiar with the rescue and its adoption policies and practices. You will get many questions on the process and, while you aren't expected to be able to answer all questions, you should understand the basics, including where to find the adoption application and the fees for adoption.

You may need to familiarize yourself with the rescue's adoption agreement. Rarely was there a representative from the rescue with me when a dog was being picked up by the adopter. This meant I had to walk people through the agreement and ensure they understood it before it was signed. I also had to collect the adoption money. If you aren't comfortable with this, ensure you discuss this in advance.

You should also be clear on requirements for spay and neuter. Many rescues make this mandatory as part of the adoption and will require the adopter to provide evidence of compliance within a certain timeframe. Note: unless the rescue arranged to spay a female dog itself, or it was a surrender with a spay

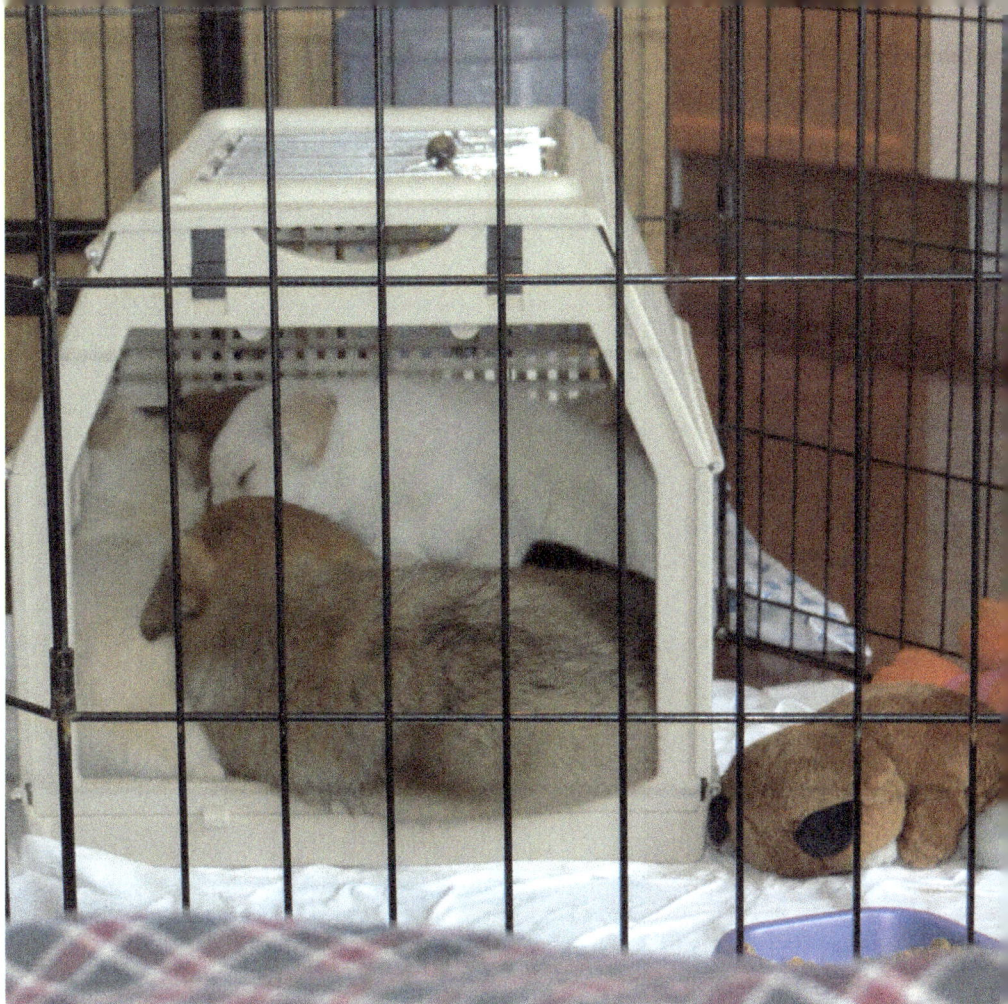

certificate, it is almost impossible to know if she has been spayed or not. I have seen some rescues charge the full adoption fee for a female and, if determined at the vet the spay had been done previously, the rescue would reimburse the adopter for the difference. It is good to find out their policies around this.

Some rescues will not have an animal spayed or neutered until it is with the adoptive family. The reasons vary, but often it is because taking care of an animal post-surgery is best done in an adoptive home rather than a foster environment. Adoption fees usually include a vet check and the spay/neuter, so it is a good opportunity for the adopter to connect with the vet clinic and learn more about the new pet, its health, and its care.

Finally, try not to provide your personal contact information if possible. I learned this lesson after being the unfortunate recipient of an angry phone call from a family that had wanted to adopt but were turned down by the rescue and they were calling me to ask me why.

Blog: Smart ... not so smart ...

I woke with a start this morning ... I realized I had slept through the night. I remember this same feeling of bliss and fear when my daughters were newborns. The euphoria of having a decent night's sleep ... and the fear of OMIGAWD WHAT'S WRONG??????

As I ventured downstairs, they were still quiet. Did the extra blanket over their kennel smother them? Or did it muffle the noise so I wasn't able to hear them? I lifted the cover and they were all eagerly bouncing at the kennel door, but not as loud as I am used to. Then ... there was ... the noise.

It was a weird, low, quiet croaky, moaning sound. It seemed to be coming from Vlad, who was just sitting there waiting to exit the kennel to do his business and get some breakfast.

Did he bark and cry so loud and so long through the night that I broke his poor puppy bark??? Oh I am such a bad puppy momma! Then he moved.

I saw then that the croaky, moaning noise came from a toy frog that had a sound box of which I was not previously aware, and Vlad had simply stepped on it.

Puppy barks and enthusiasm soon had me realize that all was well and that they were just finally settling into an overnight sleep routine.

Smart ... not so smart ...

Smart: the first one to figure out how to go down the steps off the deck into the yard was .... (drumroll) ... VESPA!

Really? you're surprised? Seriously???

Not so smart: her three brothers whining on the deck trying to figure out how to get down to where Vespa is obviously having the time of her life.

Smart: realizing that the puppies will eventually figure out how to get off the deck and going around yard to ensure there aren't any places for them (read: Vespa) to get out.

Not so smart: not blocking off deck so puppies can't get down and into the still wet and kinda muddy (read: poopy) spring yard.

Smart: putting the not-so-smart puppies down into the yard to experience the world and have more room to burn off more energy.

Not so smart: realizing that there are four puppies currently discovering every section of the yard with mud, dirt, and big dog poop.

Adoption Events

In addition to meet and greets at your home, another strategy rescues use is adoption events. These can take place anywhere, but usually in pet-friendly places like pet supply stores. They are often advertised on social media and at the store itself so anyone interested in adopting can come to see the dogs available at the event rather than going to someone's home.

If you're prepared for meet and greets, then you'll be fine at the adoption event – except it is usually a lot more chaotic – especially if there are other dogs and pups at the event. I remember taking Victor and Vespa to an event with pups from another litter that were about the same age. Any leash training was forgotten as they all wanted to play and check things out. It was a lot of fun and they were definitely tired afterwards.

Adoption events are a great way to get exposure for your foster and for the rescue. You play an important role representing both so take it seriously. Dress appropriately, be friendly, and be prepared. It really can be a lot of fun and a great way to meet people.

And if you're really good, all this hard work will pay off, and then you have to do the hardest part: saying goodbye.

Blog: Growing up … and goodbyes …

It's been a little busy around here lately. After dealing with the worms (gag), we started into full-blown "prepare puppies for adoption mode." After hearing the rescue organizer explain the process for housebreaking to a potential-adoptive family, I figured I could help start the process.

Truth be told, I did have my own selfish reasons …

Saturday afternoon, I shut down the puppy pen downstairs and brought the kennel up into our living room so the puppies would become part of the family. I removed all newspaper and opened the door to the deck.

Okay, kids … let's learn about doing business outside.

Gotta love dogs and their natural instincts. The pups always were curious about going outside and playing, so rather than keeping them from going out, we now moved into "please, for the love of all that is good and decent in the world, pleeeease go outside!" Mission accomplished.

We let the pups play around the house and have access to go outside at will – I just wish we had proper April weather because it is a little chilly in here with the door open. When the door is closed, they are starting to give cues they want to go out, including going up to the door – awesome.

The nights are a charming experience. We went to bed at 10 p.m. after having let them out to have their pre-bedtime constitutional. Sarge and I woke to the sound of barking puppies just after midnight. He promptly got up, let them out, they looked out the door, turned around and peed on the floor. Oh boy. Messes cleaned, puppies herded back into kennel, back to sleep. Well, for another two hours.

This time I got up and had a bit more success in explaining that they were still expected to go outside even if it was a little dark and cold. Little snack, little bit of water, minimal play, and they were quickly herded back into bed.

It was around 4:30 when they got up again. We were going to try and ignore them, but responsibility took over and they were once again quickly led outside. Back to bed … this time until almost 7 a.m.

Okay, we're both a little sleep deprived, but extremely grateful that the workload has reduced substantially. It's not much work at all to pick up little puppy poops (that still have the occasional worm – gag) off the deck and not having to pick up pee-soaked newspaper.

Goodbyes

Now that the pups have reached eight weeks, it's time for them to move on into their own homes.

The first to go was Vanhalen. He was a tough one for us, being the first to go and because we were so fond of him. He is such a neat little guy. But his new family is awesome and have already shared updates. He is settling in nicely and doing really well. We're so happy for them.

Vixen's adoption was finalized on Sunday and she has also gone on to her new home and is prepared to be spoiled. She has a good life coming her way as well.

Tomorrow Violet will go be with her new dog brother and start her new life. I know she will be loved as well, such a sweet little girl.

Vlad also had a great meet and greet on Sunday, and is a home check away from going to his new fur-ever home. Vaughn's potential family was having a home check tonight and we are just waiting to hear the outcome.

If those two go through, then all that are left are Valentina, Vespa and Victor. They are all wonderful dogs. Yes, Vespa is a little bundle of energy, but she is smart and obedient and learning quickly. Victor is a smart little guy who has a calm nature. Consider taking them together – they balance each other perfectly and will make for a lovely puppy family.

I'm pretty sure I'm taking this harder than Valentina, but she is starting to notice that when she comes in from outside that there is a baby missing. I contemplate what scenario would be better, slowly missing puppies, or having her go before they are taken away, but I think we would be better helping her with separation than if she went elsewhere. But it's hard to say what goes through a dog's mind. Whatever is best for her will happen. And we know we will find her the perfect home.

7 Saying Goodbye

How to cope when your fosters are adopted ... and returned

Blog: Growing up ... and goodbyes ...

Dog math can be fuzzy sometimes. I am a victim of it myself. Don't ask me how many dogs I have because I will give you a complicated answer that is meant to confuse you intentionally for reasons I will not discuss here.

When the post went up to foster a momma dog and a litter of seven puppies, it stated "a couple of weeks." We are into our third week with the pups and have them until they reach eight weeks. Dog math.

Even more confusing was trying to remember their birth date. When you're caught in the middle of puppy chaos, you take words as facts. Dog math.

In all the confusion of everything, I was told the v-litter pups were born March 5th. This meant it would be the end of April before they were eight weeks and ready to go to their new homes. But last night, as I posted new photos to their albums, I came to realize they were born February 25th, a week earlier.

That means they will reach eight weeks – and be ready to go to their new homes – on April 22nd. A whole week or more earlier than previously thought.

Dog math.

Now I will admit I'm exhausted. I am anxious to have my house back. Anyone who knows me knows that I like a clean house. That I can only enter my basement wearing rubber gloves and rubber boots should suggest I am not in my comfort zone. Being a foster to a litter of puppies is not for the weak of heart. I did this willingly, knowing that it was going to get pretty intense for someone who takes pride in a clean home (think "Monica" from the t.v. show "Friends").

I am not saying this to scare off future potential fosters – I'm just telling it the way it is. It is a lot of work, a lot of mess, and you have to be prepared. But they also bring a lot of fun and joy. I absolutely do not regret any of this for a second.

But now that I do the dog math, I realize that I only have maybe 11 days left with Valley and her pups. I see her snuggle and play with them and I realize that they will soon be separated and into their new forever homes. And I won't lie. It makes me cry a little bit. Ok. A lot. But when I see the families that are taking them in, I know that they will be given the best possible homes and that I did everything I could to prepare them for their new life.

Despite the work, the smell, being a puppy chew toy, and exceeding my garbage limit, I am going to appreciate the last 11 days I have with Valley and the pups. Because I knew going in this was temporary, and that eventually they would all be separated into different homes.

But I'm still going to cry a little. Ok. More than a little. That's dog math.

How to cope when your fosters are adopted

Unless you had a horrible foster experience or you discovered you dislike animals more than your in-laws, chances are you are going to be pretty sad to see your foster go to a new home.

I wish I could give you some tried and true method to make it easier, but the only thing I can say is that it isn't easy, I don't think it gets easier, and I don't think it is supposed to get easier. All it means is that you are a good and caring person and the perfect foster.

From the outset, I kept reminding myself that fostering was temporary, that one day Valley and her pups would be going to new homes. Homes. Plural. Honestly, I think that was the toughest part, watching her puppies leave one by one with a different family each time. I was a tearful mess before, during, and after, every single time. Poor Terry.

I think the most difficult was when Valley started noticing that some of her puppies were missing and she would be looking around for them. It was at that point that I knew we had to find her a new home sooner than later because it would break my heart for her to be the last, wandering around, wondering where all her puppies went. (Okay, I *may* have been more emotional than she would have been.)

We also had to consider the brat pack, who was also accustomed to having Valley and the pups around and realizing the herd was slowly decreasing in size. We tried to make the best of it for all of us.

So we played.

We played in the backyard, we played at the off leash park. We chased, we ran, we threw balls, we hugged, we smooshed little puppy faces, we took pictures, and we had fun. When the family came to pick up their new friend – or in some instances we delivered – we knew we had the best time possible on our last day with them.

The important thing, though was to keep Valentina out of sight when the family came to pick up the pup as we didn't want her to start associating people with her puppies going missing and start to get protective. It also made it easier for the adopters to not see her sad face.

Blog: Dog Math Part III

We're missing a dog.

Seriously. We're missing her.

Last night, we dropped Valentina off at her forever home. Rather than having the family pick her up as we have traditionally done, we instead took her for a car ride so we could introduce her to her new home and new family, hopefully making it easier for her to settle in.

We knew when we met them that they were the perfect family. That feeling was reaffirmed when we drove up and the older daughter was standing at the door, waiting most impatiently for us to arrive. When we pulled up, I waved, and saw the sheer excitement on her face. Her dog was coming home.

This family is awesome and amazing and I know they will love her as much – or even more – than we did. Even more exciting was Valley's reaction to the cats – meaning no reaction, aside from perhaps being a little leary of them. All in all, everything went as it should.

It was tough leaving Valley behind, especially when she came following us to the door, looking expectantly at Sarge to open the door and we would all go through together. I brought her back to her new forever mom, told her to hold Valley, be firm with her, be the new alpha in Valley's life, as Valley will connect with her first.

We left, tried not to look back, and went home to the brat pack and the two remaining pups.

Before taking Valley to her new home, we did take her, the pups, and the brat pack to the off leash park for one last romp together. And they took full advantage of it. All of them – even the pups – have great recall. Well except when Vespa totally got distracted by another dog and didn't want to leave.

Valentina, along with assistance from the brat pack, has raised some very well-rounded, curious and confident pups.

But we miss Valley. Shawn the Super Schnauzer especially. He hasn't been right since she left. Although I wonder if he's afraid that, after watching all these dogs disappear, he might be next. He has nothing to fear from me, although Sarge may be looking for someone to take him and Beanie in so we can keep Vespa and Victor …

Dog Math … 4+8-1-1-1-1+1-1-1 = 6.

… and returned

Despite everything – caring for your foster, doing the right training, the rescue doing the appropriate screening and approval process - things can happen and a dog you thought found a new home ends up back at your door. This very quickly becomes public information as the rescue now needs to find a new home for the pet. One thing I have learned over the years as social media has progressed is that people – particularly people passionate about something, like animals – will have strong opinions and will not hesitate to voice them.

Likely, the criticism will not be directed at you because, generally, people look at fosters as being superheroes in the animal rescue world. It's a cool position to be in, but you can also expect more scrutiny of your words and actions. But it is also your opportunity to use your powers for good and try to calm the masses and bring some perspective to the situation.

Blog: Dog Math Part II

Last Friday night, my extended family of a momma and seven pups dropped down to momma and two pups.

But Dog Math reared its head and, within less than a week, I was back up to momma and three pups. Yes, Vlad returned back to the nest.

This was announced on the rescue's Facebook page and there were some comments about how quickly he came back. But it is easy to speak when the full circumstances aren't known.

I know the family, and I know that taking on a puppy was not a frivolous decision. It was a fully thought-out decision. Vlad was well-suited for them. They were fully prepared to take responsibility for him and incorporate him as an important part of their family.

Unfortunately, health issues reared their ugly heads and it made the situation difficult. It wasn't allergies or anything that could have been predicted.

I respect the decision the family made. It may seem to some that Vlad was given up easily, but he was brought back to his foster home with open arms, from me, his momma, the brat pack, and Vespa and Victor.

He is a beautiful dog, already knows his name, sits on command, comes when called, and is a true gentleman. Five days with the family were five well-spent days. Rather than allowing him to be in a situation that could end up negatively affecting him, he was brought back to a home where he will stay until he finds the perfect home.

I worry more for Kermit, a toy that was brought back with Vlad, who was the unfortunate victim of a three-way tug of war between Vlad, Vespa and Valley.

Right now, I have Vlad sleeping at my feet, two schnauzers snoring on the couch, Victor sprawled on the dog bed, Vespa in the kennel with Sport (which is amazing as Sport has been anti-puppy from day 1 and only recently started playing with them) and watching Cosmo standing over Valley, protecting her as she rests.

Don't do the dog math. All I know is that there is a bunch of beautiful, loving dogs in my home, all of whom have somehow figured out how to live together. I can't keep them all, no matter how much I want to, but I know that for Valley and her babies, their future is yet to be written.

But please, people ... we are starting demo and renovations on our house this weekend. For the love of all that is good and decent in the world, please don't make us do this with all these dogs in the house!!!

Social media has evolved in many ways, and, sadly, is many times a platform of personal opinions, heated discussion, disagreement, and negativity. But during the time we fostered, social media was a godsend for us and still continues to be our link to our fostering past.

We were fortunate enough to have connected with the family who adopted Valentina, as well as those who adopted Vixen, Victor and Vespa, and VanHalen. My only regret is that I didn't do so for those who adopted Vaughn, Vlad, and Violet. I really would love to see how they turned out, especially Violet and Vlad and their beautiful sable coats, or how big Vaughn got, having been the biggest of the litter.

Perhaps this book will be one way to reach out to them, have them contact me, and we can coordinate a big family reunion. I think that would be a great way to help me get past some of the disappointment and anger I have from when everything with the rescue went bad.

Blog: Déjà vu …

Yay! It's spring!! After what seemed like an endless winter, spring has finally arrived in Alberta. For us, this means home renovation time – clearing out old furniture, stripping out flooring to replace with new, and repainting the whole house.

This was a project we had planned for the spring before we agreed to foster Valley and the pups. Indeed, the timing was perfect – why not foster now when we are going to rip everything out and replace it later anyway?

Well, as said before, our two week foster is coming up on two months. Not that we have an issue with that. We know that the rescue has had to deal with a lot of animals coming in, emergency rescues, foster home shortages, etc. With four pups adopted out, it is less chaotic and more routine.

Vespa, Victor and Vlad pretty much sleep through the night, waking usually only if the brat pack wakes up and decides they need to go out in the middle of the night. They go into their kennel by themselves in the evening, usually by 9:00 p.m., and will sleep until 6, 7 if they got up once through the night.

Valley continues to sleep in our room, although with the warmer weather, it is harder to convince her to come inside in the evenings when it is so beautifully cool outside. But she has learned what "bed time!" means and will come scrambling up the stairs with the others. She sleeps quietly on the floor at the foot of the bed and lives in happy contentment.

It is that contentment that makes her such a great family dog. And it is that contentment that helped a prospective family fall in love with her during a meet-and-greet Friday evening. We are crossing our fingers and waiting with bated breath to find out whether Valley's adoption is a go. We love Valentina and would adopt her in a heartbeat, but she deserves a family where she can be the star, not another member of the brat pack.

Vlad was also a star this weekend, and had his very own meet-and-greet on Saturday. It went so well that, not only was there shared affection between them and Vlad, but it seemed that the brat pack was quite willing to go home with them as well. We took Vlad to their place Sunday for a meet-and-greet with their dog, and not only did it go very well, but Sarge and I were hinting for them to adopt us as well.

And we are still waiting for Victor and Vespa to find their own homes – like, seriously, how are these two not adopted yet? If you saw Vespa and Victor chasing ice cubes around the kitchen, you would scoop them up in a heartbeat! It was the funniest thing ever!

When two weeks turn to two months - or more

Managing when your rescue relationship goes bad

Blog: What the heck just happened??

It was the weirdest thing. Sarge and I were on our way to Wetaskiwin last night to check out the restaurant/bar that Sarge's cousin and his fiancee own. As we were enjoying the quiet drive, we both had this weird moment of awareness. What the heck just happened?

March 23rd, a mere five weeks ago, life took an entirely different direction for us. We opened our home to Valentina and her litter of seven puppies and suddenly that consumed our lives. We were knee deep in puppy poop, mixing up tubs of pumpkin-yogurt-cottage cheese puppy mush, opening our house to meet and greets, taking puppies to vets, cleaning, cleaning, cleaning, giving up on cleaning, and preparing puppies to go off to their new homes and new lives.

Last night Vlad went to his new home and he was the last with an adoption pending. Our house has gone from Valley and a litter of seven to Valley, Victor and Vespa. And it's quiet.

Vespa and Victor are certainly playful and energetic, but they are good puppies, very sweet, very smart, and affectionate. They were two of the first to be housebroken and they were the first two to figure out how to get down the steps to the yard. And they make full use of that skill as they race around the yard, burning off all that puppy energy. They go immediately to the kennel to nap and are pretty much sleeping through the night.

They are going to grow up into a couple of great dogs.

But Valley is having her own "what the heck just happened" moment, as after Vlad left last night, she has really noticed that she is missing a significant number of puppies and was wandering around the house last night looking for them. Poor girl.

She is such a great momma and did a wonderful job with her pups. Let's find this girl her own home as well where she can be loved and cherished.

Managing when your rescue goes bad

While this book is intended to be entertainment, it is also about helping people interested in fostering animals have the right information going into it and keeping the experience and relationship positive. It's also a guide book for rescues to consider their operations and ensure they do the right things to have the best possible relationship with their foster volunteers.

Anyone who followed my blog would have noticed it dropped off rather abruptly. Last anyone heard, we still had two puppies – Victor and Vespa – who had not yet been adopted. They were still being promoted on the site, but no more blog posts. What happened?

As I mentioned at the outset, ours was only to be a temporary foster, two weeks at best. As the rescue struggled to find a new foster home, we agreed to keep Valley and her pups longer. We were happy to do it. We believed that, once the puppies were old enough to go to new homes, it wouldn't take long for them to all be adopted out. If anything, we were more concerned that Valentina would take longer to be adopted.

Weeks passed and, before we knew it, April was gone and suddenly it was May. I had to go away on business in June and Terry was coming with me. We raised this with the rescue organizer – numerous times - confirming the dates we would be gone and would need someone to take care of the puppies while we were gone (we had enough to worry about finding a place for our own dogs).

As the date drew closer, it became harder and harder to reach the rescue organizer. She was known for "going off the grid" and ignoring Facebook messages, texts, and phone calls. Her voice mailbox was full and she was essentially missing in action.

Sadly, I wasn't the only one frustrated by this, as other fosters were having issues as well. The poor rescue volunteers were taking the brunt of the frustration from all of us, but were helpless. They had no more luck in reaching her than we did.

With no leader in sight, and seeing our desperation, one of the volunteers came forward and said she would find a temporary foster to watch Victor and Vespa while we were away. A call was put out, people responded, and soon we were connected with another family who would watch the pups while we were gone. The evening before we were set to leave, we went to their home with the pups, their kennel, blankets, food, dishes, and favourite toys. I gave them my number to contact me if they had any issues, and left thinking everything was good to go.

We were so wrong.

The next day, I received a phone call from the rescue organizer, blasting me for dropping off the dogs at an unapproved foster home, especially one that had kids, that the dogs were terrified, messing in the house, and I was in big trouble.

What the what???

A few more exchanges occurred, both by telephone and text message, before I finally emailed my resignation as a foster for that rescue effective immediately. Terry and I left for our trip with our hearts broken, especially since we never got to say goodbye to Victor and Vespa, and would likely never see them again.

If you go back to the first chapter and the conversation about foster agreements, I am sure you can now see why all that information was included. If I knew then what I know now, I think things would have gone significantly different. But, then again, maybe I wouldn't have ended up fostering and would have lost out on the experience of having Valley and her babies as part of our lives. I wouldn't have given that up for the world.

I was told afterwards what I did – dropping the pups off – was in fact in contravention of the agreement because the person who approved the temporary foster did not have the authority to do so. I was also required to provide notice of my resignation, which makes sense as a rescue would need more than an hour's notice to find a new home for a dog - or dogs.

The disorganization of the rescue worked to my advantage and they neglected to have me or Terry sign a foster agreement. Unfortunately, it also meant that we had no means of being reimbursed for all our expenses, including canned pumpkin, cottage cheese, dog food, puppy food, and more. We wrote it all off as a loss and a lesson learned, a valuable and expensive one from which you can benefit.

I don't think I am the only one to ever have had a bad experience like this, but I get the sense that, over time, animal rescues have matured and evolved and are getting much better.

That said, dear reader, I implore you, whether you are considering fostering, are already fostering, or are a rescue that deals with fosters, go back to Chapter 1 and read through again and make sure all is in order. Rescues play such an important role in saving animals and giving them a second chance at a good life. The relationship between rescues and volunteers are critical to success. Working together, we can all save more of these precious lives.

Blog: Babies grow up so fast … *sigh*

Yay! It's spring!! After what seemed like an endless winter, spring has It's been two weeks since Valentina and the V-litter have come into our lives and wow, the changes in all of them is surreal.

Valentina is starting to fill out, particularly since she isn't nursing as much and can actually keep the nutrition on her body rather than feeding the pups.

The puppies, I swear, have doubled in size. All you have to do is look at the picture of them nursing the first day and then the other day, and you can see the difference!

Most amusing is their coordination. They all used to stumble around like they had one too many beers at the pub (well, except Vespa who bounced drunkenly …). Now they all run, mostly in packs, and usually to attack my ankles or to chase down one of the brat pack.

Okay, that's not true. They don't really run. They certainly don't walk. They actually bounce and pounce. It's like there's little springs in their chubby little legs. Vespa and Victor are particularly springy. Although Vespa stood out at first as being the smart one, Victor is quickly showing himself to be a bold and intelligent young fella. It's becoming more apparent that Victor and Vespa have the same dad, as they have the same slender physique. Both will be smart, active, and athletic dogs. Oh, I wish I could keep these two.

Then there's Vanhalen and Vaughn, both bigger boys, quiet yet playful. They're stockier little guys, and remind me of fuzzy blonde teddy bears. I was very happy to hear a wonderful family has chosen Vanhalen and

---

are only a homecheck and three weeks away from bringing him into their home. I'm happy and yet sad – oh I wish I could keep these two.

Violet and Vlad always make me laugh. Their sable colour, their sweet brown eyes, their little smile inherited from Valley … and their quiet and not-so-quiet determination! Violet always had some spunk to her, just like her sisters. Vlad is coming into his own and is pretty hilarious. He is a momma's boy, and has been known to fall alseep curled up to her, sometimes using her tail as a pillow. He is also hell-bent on getting onto the couch downstairs. He even backed up under the coffee table and took a running start to try and get up. No luck, but as fast as he is growing, I almost expect him to be able to climb up on the couch within a week. Violet and Vlad, the little sable teddy bears. Oh, I wish I could keep these two.

Then there's our little Vixen. Still the smallest of the litter, she has become quite precocious, and can often be found attacking her mother's tail. There is an adoption pending for her and looking forward to hearing if it has been finalized or not. I almost hope not – oh, how I wish I could keep her.

The best part is seeing how Valley is responding to having time away from the pups and how they all interact when together. Valley is playing with the pups more and it is hilarious. I laughed so hard today I almost dropped my camera. I tried to take a video, but when Valley turned Vespa onto her back and was playing with her, I had to put the camera down, I was crying.

Oh, and they're starting to dream. Just now, Vaughn apparently had one where he was running to Edmonton or chasing a schnauzer, but his little legs were going for about two minutes. I almost woke him up, I was laughing so hard …

9 ♥ Happily Ever After

If you've been paying attention, you know that our story didn't end when we left Victor and Vespa so we could go on our trip.

Thankfully, I remained friends with some of the volunteers, and we soon learned that Valentina's last two puppies found a home together, which was the best we could ever have asked for them. But our hearts were still broken and we were very angered by the whole situation with the rescue, particularly how we were treated and disrespected after everything went down.

The year we fostered was also the year Terry and I were getting married, so once we had our home back to ourselves with only the brat pack to worry about, we were able to get back to renovating to sell the duplex and planning our September wedding (I think you can guess who focused on which part of that task list).

It was maybe a week before the wedding, and I was meeting with my sister, my niece, and my kids to go through some final details for the Big Day. As I drove through the parking lot to the restaurant where we were meeting, I saw a man and a woman get out of a car with two white dogs. Two very familiar white dogs.

I threw my car in park, and ran out towards them, my kids staring wide-eyed, wondering if their mother had lost her mind. I called out to the couple, hopeful and shaking, "is that Victor and Vespa?"

The couple – somewhat startled and leary - responded that yes, it was them.

My heart racing, tears welling up in my eyes, I asked if I could come say hi to them, and then quickly explained who I was. At that point, Victor and Vespa were already bouncing at the ends of their leashes towards me as they recognized me. The couple graciously agreed and I got to give hugs and kisses and see that Victor and Vespa were, in fact, doing good, they were happy and healthy, and they were together.

It was the best wedding gift I could ever receive.

Serendipity continued on my side, as it happened my stepsister knew one of them from high school and they were friends on Facebook. Connections were made and we are all still connected today.

Good things do happen to good people.

One promise I made to those I kept in touch with is that we would always try to make ourselves available to dog sit for any of them when they needed, and we have been taken up on that offer many times. We live on an acreage now, so we have much more room for them to play and it is a joy to continue to have them in our lives. My sister has Vixen, and every time I see her, she loses her mind, she is so excited to see me. Valentina has bonded very closely with her family and looks so sad when they drop her off. But she quickly connects with Terry, her first love, and all is good. Victor and Vespa live on their own acreage now and are having the time of their lives being spoiled and burning off all that beautiful energy.

Will we foster again? Probably.

First, we would need to get the yard fenced as we have too many open areas and too many temptations in our subdivision, including goats, cows and horses.

Second, our brat pack, still intact with a new addition, Lily, is getting older. They did a wonderful job helping socialize Valley and the pups. But it can be stressful and too much attention taken away from them. With three of four original brat pack as seniors heading into twilight years, they deserve all of our love right now.

Finally, we need to prepare ourselves for fostering, including our lives and especially our home, which is in a state of perpetual renovation. When we do it again, we will be ready to give it our all.

And we will be prepared.

So this is the end of our fostering story – for now.

Victor and Vespa during one of their visits to our acreage.

Vixen loses her mind everytime she sees me and still listens to Terry better than anyone.

A friend saw this picture on Facebook and said "that is what happy looks like." After hearing of Terry's heart attack, some of the adoptive families pulled together to arrange a visit at the off-leash park to help cheer me up. VanHalen is making sure I am feeling the love.

Reunion at the off-leash park, including Victor, Vespa, Valley, and the brat pack. Here, Victor is saying hi to his momma. (Shawn is just looking for attention from anyone)

Vanhalen catching a snooze, while Vixen and Valentine enjoy some playtime

Vlad and Vespa during a meet and greet
Vlad's turn for playtime with Valentina

Lightning Source UK Ltd.
Milton Keynes UK
UKOW06f1432250817

307896UK00009B/82/P